GHOSTS
IN
THE
MACHINE

GHOSTS

IN THE

Overcoming
Decision-Making
Biases in the
Sales Cycle with
Behavioral Science

MACHINE

Ryan Voeltz

ISBN Hardcover: 978-1-7373515-2-8
ISBN Paperback: 978-1-7373515-1-1
ISBN Electronic: 978-1-7373515-0-4
Library of Congress Control Number: 2021915756

Portions of this book are works of nonfiction. Certain names and identifying characteristics have been changed.

Printed in the United States of America.

REV Press
PO Box 2447
Livermore, CA 94551-2447

www.RyanVoeltz.com

This book is dedicated to my family.

To my parents, Bruce and Doralyn, who had the greatest influence on making me the person I am today. Thank you for teaching me the importance of fairness, laughter, humility, and education.

To my sister, Kelly, who is a better person than I am. Thank you for inspiring me to be a kinder, gentler, and happier version of myself.

To my wife, Tara, who is the best partner I could ever hope for. Thank you for picking up the slack while I pursued this little passion project.

And to my children, Caroline and Hunter, who are rays of light. Thank you for being the funniest and happiest people I've ever met.

I love you all.

CONTENTS

GHOSTS
IN
THE
MACHINE

Overcoming
Decision-Making
Biases in the
Sales Cycle with
Behavioral Science

Ryan Voeltz

PREFACE

There it was, staring me in the face. Four hundred and fifty-five pounds.

There I was, lying on the bench, gearing myself up to lift this ridiculous amount of weight. I weigh 195 pounds, and before this I had never bench-pressed more than 245.

I was about to attempt a single unassisted repetition—pick this thing up, lower it down to my chest, and press it back up—which would basically double my previous personal best. This is not something that should be possible. And that was exactly what I thought, too, before I learned one particular secret about lifting really heavy weights.

What had seemed impossible before...

...was now still very much impossible.

This absurd little bench-press story never happened. It could *never* happen, because there is no secret to lifting really heavy weight. No shortcuts.[1] Nobody has ever been able or will ever be able to use a secret shortcut to double their weight-lifting performance overnight.

If you want to lift really heavy weights, all you have to do is lift progressively heavier amounts of weight consistently over time.[2] Progressive overload—as in, progressively increasing your workload—is well-known in fitness circles as the way to build strength and lift heavier weight. It is not a secret.

And just like there is no one magical secret to lifting heavy weights, there is no one particular secret to being a successful salesperson.

If you came here to discover "secrets" or "shortcuts" to being a successful salesperson, you have come to the wrong place. This is not that kinda book. This is a *why* book.

Value that comes from secrets and shortcuts is fleeting; value that comes from *why* has staying power.

This book will help you understand *why* you see and experience the same patterns and challenges throughout the sales process. In doing so, it will provide you with a solid foundation of knowledge about yourself and the human beings you are selling to that you may rely on as you work to sustain success over time.

Let me make something clear right from the jump: *Ghosts in the Machine* is not an attempt to recreate the sales wheel.

There are plenty of sales methodologies—from Solution Selling to Consultative Selling to SPIN®-Selling—that are

---

1 Steroids aside

2 *Of course* some methods of doing this are better and more efficient than others, but, fundamentally, all resistance training programs leverage the progressive overload principle. This is not debated.

proven successful approaches in converting prospects into customers. Instead of replacing your preferred sales methodology, the discussion in the following pages focuses on gaining a better understanding of the people to whom you are selling, and the hidden drivers behind the decisions they make throughout the sales cycle, by leveraging insights from behavioral science.

THIS BOOK IS FOR YOU

No matter where you are in your sales career, this book is for you.

If you are a new salesperson, this book offers a guiding light for how to interact and communicate with the various decision-makers you will encounter on your sales journey. Further, this approach will integrate seamlessly with just about any specific, tactical training that your company provides.

If you are an underperforming salesperson, whether early or late in your sales career, this book provides a better understanding of the people you have been interacting with and how to approach them more confidently and effectively. Most underperforming salespeople are capable of excelling but have yet to find an approach that works for them. I believe that the behavioral science approach may be the key to unlock that potential.

If you are a successful salesperson, this book offers novel insights that will push you to the next level of success. This book presents the sales cycle through a different frame, providing clarity and definition to patterns you will probably recognize but perhaps have yet to articulate. A new lens on these patterns can only make you all the more effective in working with your prospects and customers. Further, the behavioral approach may be just what you need to finally break through with those few stubborn prospects that do not seem interested in picking up what you are putting down.

Even if you are not formally employed as a salesperson—maybe you are a founding member of a startup company interested in exploring opportunities in new markets, or maybe you are a corporate executive or manager tasked with leading a cross-functional organizational change, or maybe you would simply like to be more persuasive in "selling" your ideas in a professional setting—this book gives you a practical blueprint for connecting with people and positioning your ideas in ways that will resonate with your intended audience.

Whether you are new to sales, underperforming, crushing it, or somewhere in between, I am supremely confident that the following pages hold insights that will resonate with you and help you along your sales journey. And if you are coming at this whole sales thing from another angle altogether, there will be plenty here for you, too.

UNDERSTANDING WHY

Real success in sales—or anything for that matter—requires sustained and consistent effort over time.

Period.

That said, understanding *why* certain phases of the sales cycle tend to unfold the way they do, why the same patterns and challenges emerge, will add tremendous value to those sustained and consistent efforts. Understanding why things happen the way they do will enable you to become more efficient and effective as you strive for success; understanding will motivate you to apply your efforts in ways that will move the needle rather than waste your time. Understanding why something works increases the odds that you will be able to figure out how to succeed in approaching it, regardless of the exact details.

If you have been selling for any amount of time, you have likely had the experience of working hard to convince someone of the value of your product or service, only to have your message fall on deaf ears. You try throwing every selling point you have at the wall, and yet nothing seems to stick.

Then, one way or another, you learn what is really important to that person—their *why*, the reason behind their decision-making process. Suddenly, while you are still working just as hard as you did before, you are able to make progress, align your value prop with their desires, and breeze through the rest of the sales process.

In these situations, the difference between failure and success is not in how hard you work. It is not necessarily making better use of a given sales methodology. And it definitely is not in leveraging some secret or shortcut. The difference is in understanding why, because understanding why allows you to choose courses of action that will help you turn your efforts into achievements. That is what this book is about.

Ghosts in the Machine is about the *whys* behind the common challenges salespeople encounter at each phase in the sales cycle. Instead of promising secrets and shortcuts for success or recreating the sales wheel, this book will help you understand why the challenges you face persist. In doing so, the guidance herein will work alongside your preferred sales methodology, whatever it may be. Along the way we will uncover plenty of really good *hows*—not secrets, but proven and effective strategies—but they are not nearly as important as the *whys*.

EMBRACING IRRATIONALITY

Society in general, and the sales profession in particular, operates under a few basic assumptions about people— one being that we are all basically rational and guided by strictly logical thought processes. Lots of philosophy and historical scholarship has been focused on this idea.

However, in the last hundred or so years, as our understanding of the human animal has improved dramatically, it has become clear that we still have a relatively tenuous grip on why people do the things they do. And the more we learn about ourselves, the more we are realizing that while "rational and logical" sounds good, it is just not an accurate description of how people act in the real world.

People deviate from doing what is rational in a wide variety of circumstances. The sales process is no exception. However, for some reason, most sales training is still based on the assumption of rational behavior. Sales organizations assume that salespeople and their prospects and customers can be counted on to make rational decisions.

In this book, I combine my experience as a salesperson with my passion for behavioral science, and I argue that *predictably irrational*[3] behavior might be the most underappreciated aspect of sales, and that it leaves a substantial imprint on each stage of the sales cycle.

Pretty much every part of the sales process, from

---

3   to borrow a phrase from the as-such-titled Dan Ariely book

prospecting to negotiating and closing, has been thoroughly dissected in countless books and training programs. Every part, it seems, *except* the impact of human irrationality on all of it. This remains a blind spot for most sales organizations. It also represents a huge opportunity.

Behavioral science (including the headline-hogging branch of behavioral economics) provides wonderful insights into these innate human irrationalities and their impact on decision-making. Embracing these principles as equal to those of more broadly accepted theories about rational decision-making will provide sales organizations with an advantage in the marketplace.

According to John Fleming and James Harter of the Gallup organization, authors of a report on applying behavioral science to drive growth and profitability, "substantial gains in performance based on attention to neoclassical economic metrics are relatively unlikely" and "applied behavioral economics—holds the promise of realizing breakthrough improvements in employee productivity, customer retention, and real growth and profitability."[4]

By applying behavioral science principles to the different phases of the sales cycle, I hope to shed light on some important and underappreciated factors that can have a dramatic impact your success.

WHO AM I?

Nearly every job I have had in my life has been a sales job.

When I was in college, I sold menswear at Nordstrom. In my first job out of college I sold copy machines. I have sold

4   John H. Fleming and James K. Harter, *The Next Discipline: Applying Behavioral Economics to Drive Growth and Profitability*, Gallup, September 2012, gallup.com/services/178028/next-discipline-pdf.aspx.

litigation support services, newswire distribution and web services, financial products, and driving range golf tees.

I have worked for large corporations and small businesses. I have led the sales effort for a startup. I have sold products and services. I have sold small-ticket and large-ticket items. I have sold B2C and B2B, both to C-suite executives in high-rise conference rooms and middle managers in nondescript cubicles. I have sold directly to customers and as an internal product partner. You would be hard-pressed to find a type of sales job that I have not done.

Twenty years of firsthand experience holding a wide variety of types of sales jobs had provided me with deep insight into what it takes to succeed as a salesperson— and the many difficulties and challenges that come with a sales career. Along the way, I have learned a lot about what differentiates successful salespeople from those who struggle to achieve and sustain success. I have also studied and researched many of the best-practice sales methodologies—including the ones you have likely been or will be trained in. And I have been to more sales trainings than I care to remember.

In these pages you will find all the things I wish I had known at the beginning of my sales career, as well as insights into the key lessons that I still find myself struggling with. This book represents the most important things I have learned in a career-long search to understand what it takes to be successful in sales.

It is worth mentioning that, reflecting on those times that I have achieved success in my sales career, it is clear to me that they are connected by a common thread: a passion for what I was doing. And if you want to sustain success in your role as a sales professional, you had better be passionate about it. Without passion it is too difficult to maintain the focused effort that success requires. It is too hard to keep getting back up when you get knocked down by the various unavoidable obstacles you must overcome. **Every other piece of sales success advice—including those offered in this book—is subordinate to approaching the job with passion.**

Personally, I am passionate about the idea of leveraging behavioral science to drive improvement in sales performance. I believe behavioral science offers an untapped well of concepts and principles that sales organizations have only just begun to appreciate, let alone put into practice.

Ghosts in the Machine is my attempt to add to the sales success conversation by applying some of these concepts and principles to the sales cycle in a systematic and holistic way. In doing so, I hope that I have put something together that you will find helpful on your personal journey to success.

Sincerely,

RYAN VOELTZ

INTRODUCTION

The beef short rib at Leopold's is the best kind of comfort food.

Unassuming yet inviting in presentation, it is served with braised red cabbage, cheesy mashed potatoes, and crispy onion strings. When you take a fully composed bite with a little bit of everything, all five taste sensations are teased to life in just the right way. The meat is tender without falling apart under the pressure of a fork and knife. It is juicy without being sloppy. It is perfect. So perfect that I have never wanted to try anything else on the menu.

And that is the problem.

Understanding why I would be so hesitant to order something new is the beginning of a journey that cuts right to the heart of one of the biggest misconceptions about being a salesperson: the idea that your prospects are purely rational decision-makers.

Decision-making—whether in the boardroom or at the dinner table—is a delicate dance in which both rational and irrational factors take turns leading. Unfortunately, most organizations train their salespeople to approach prospects and customers as if they were making decisions based on pure rationality. This book challenges that assumption and outlines an approach that will help you manage the myriad of irrational decision-making quirks that can derail the sales cycle.

But we are getting ahead of ourselves. Back to Leopold's.

THE *REAL* COMPETITION

In 2012 my wife and I moved to the Russian Hill neighborhood of San Francisco. Not long after the dust had settled on moving in, we headed out to explore the area and find somewhere to eat. It took us all of five minutes and two blocks to wander into Leopold's.

Leopold's is a typical Austrian-German gasthaus. It looks and feels exactly like you would expect an Austrian-German gasthaus to look and feel: communal wooden tables, waitresses in dirndls, huge steins of German-style beer, a big wooden bar anchoring the back of the restaurant, a boisterous atmosphere, and lots of vaguely Bavarian décor on the walls. It is a special place.

Among the many reasons we came to love Leopold's, their beef short rib sits at the top of the list. However, I almost missed out on the dish altogether. On that maiden visit to Leopold's, I skipped right over the short rib and ordered the schnitzel (a kind of breaded and fried pork). As luck would have it, my wife ordered the short rib.

The schnitzel was good. Given different circumstances, I'm sure I would've ordered it again. However, it only took one bite of the short rib for my wife, who is typically stingy when it comes to sharing her food, to look across the table and say, "You gotta try this." I obliged, expecting to be underwhelmed. Instead, that one bite kicked off a love affair that endures to this day.

Other than the distant memory of the schnitzel from that first visit, I have no idea what the other entrées on Leopold's menu taste like. It is possible that there are other entrées that are just as mind-blowing, but they shall remain unknown to me.

I must confess this is not really about passion for amazing food so much as it is about fear. I simply do not want to risk ordering something that is not as good as the short rib. The fear of being let down by another dish—that is, the fear of a relatively worse outcome—is what keeps bringing me back to this one delicious entrée.

It is not just me, and it does not just happen with food. This behavioral quirk impacts the lives of all human beings in a wide variety of ways.

The fear of a relatively worse outcome, which biases people toward a preference for the current state of affairs, is one of humanity's deepest instinctual biases: *the status quo bias*. That is, the assumption that the current state of affairs—a delicious short rib, for example—is preferable to a potential change.

Behavioral science research tells us the status quo bias

applies in a wide variety of contexts. One paper suggests that around 43% of our daily behaviors are performed out of habit.[5] Habits, of course, are little more than the physical manifestation of the status quo bias. If you look around, you will find the status quo bias basically everywhere.

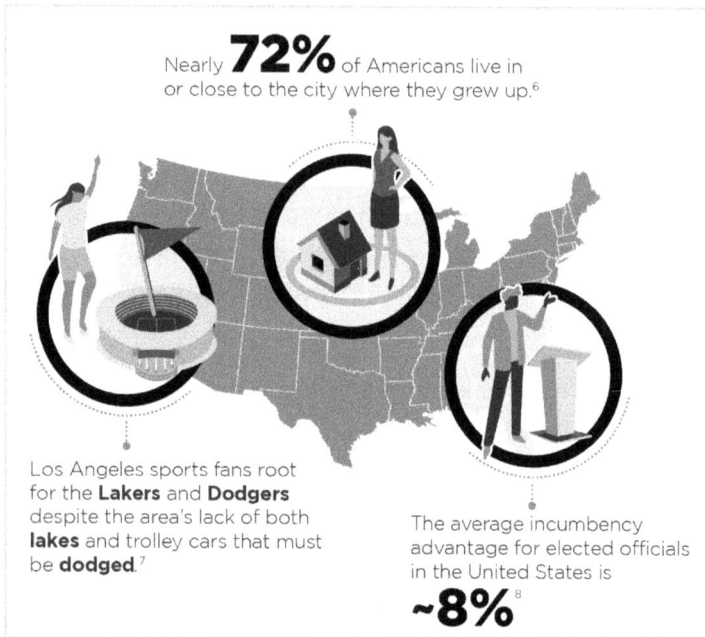

Nearly **72%** of Americans live in or close to the city where they grew up.[6]

Los Angeles sports fans root for the **Lakers** and **Dodgers** despite the area's lack of both **lakes** and trolley cars that must be **dodged**.[7]

The average incumbency advantage for elected officials in the United States is **~8%**[8]

5   Wendy Wood, Jeffrey M. Quinn, and Deborah A. Kashy, "Habits in Everyday Life: Thought, Emotion, and Action," *Journal of Personality and Social Psychology* 83, no. 6 (2002): 1281–87.

6   "What Percentage of Americans Currently Live in the Town or City Where They Grew Up?," northAmerican Moving Services, https://www.northamerican.com/infographics/where-they-grew-up.

7   Stephen Ansolabehere and James M. Snyder Jr., "The Incumbency Advantage in U.S. Elections: An Analysis of State and Federal Offices, 1942-2000," *Election Law Journal* 1, no. 3 (2002): 315–38

8   The Lakers franchise began in Minneapolis in 1947—named in honor of the "Land of 10,000 lakes"—and moved to Los Angeles in 1960; the Dodgers franchise began in Brooklyn in the 1890s—named after the danger posed by Brooklyn's new electric trolley cars—and moved to Los Angeles in 1957. The names, however, stuck.

We will dig deeper into the status quo bias later in this book. For now, we simply need to be aware that the status quo bias impacts decision-making in nearly every context of human life, from the personal to the professional.

This tendency we all have to prefer what we know over what we do not is the link between my short rib obsession and the challenge of building relationships with your prospects and converting them into paying customers. Just as I fear a different entrée will be relatively worse than the short rib, your prospects fear that a change from their status quo—whether that means switching vendors or doing something new altogether—will result in a relatively worse outcome.

Unlike in the restaurant business, where it is not an issue if customers order the same thing every time so long as they keep coming back, salespeople on the receiving end of the status quo bias experience a resistance to change from prospects and customers that presents a serious obstacle to realizing successful outcomes.

Every day, in every stage of the sales cycle, salespeople struggle to manage and overcome the resistance to change they receive from their prospects. **But contrary to popular opinion, this resistance does not primarily come from competing products or services.** Rather, resistance comes first from instinctual biases within the human thought process, biases that impact decision-making and resist change-making efforts.

The status quo bias is just one piece of the decision-making puzzle, the first of many cognitive biases that we'll be discussing in this book. However, before we go any further, let's level-set: what, exactly, is a cognitive bias?

COGNITIVE BIAS

A cognitive bias is a pattern of deviation from rational judgment. Rather than behavior being driven by an objective view of the world, an individual's subjective view—their perception of reality—tends to dictate behavior. Because this subjective view is frequently at odds with an otherwise unbiased view of reality, it may distort judgement and decision-making, driving what can appear to others to be irrational behavior.

A handful of key cognitive biases have a disproportionate impact on decision-making during the sales cycle. These critical human biases promote active resistance to the thoughtful and diligent efforts of salespeople, often in the face of objectively superior solutions. They may be all in our heads, but this group of biases are responsible for many of the very real reasons that sales can be such a difficult job.

Together, these biases represent the greatest challenge salespeople face. They are the *real* competition.

Believe it or not, success in sales does not come from objective comparisons of your offering to another product or service alone. No matter the product, service, industry, or company, sustained sales success comes primarily from understanding and effectively responding to the innate biases that influence your prospects and customers throughout the sales cycle.

"IRRATIONAL"

"Wouldn't economics make a lot more sense if it were based on how people actually behave, instead of how they should behave?"
—Dan Ariely

The cognitive bias concept, popularized by Amos Tversky and Daniel Kahneman, based on their collaborative research in the 1970s. To understand their research, however, we have to look at the ideas that came before them—ideas that have been guiding our popularly accepted explanations for human behavior for quite a long time.

One in particular stands out.

RATIONAL CHOICE THEORY

Dating back to the late eighteenth century, rational choice theory argues that human beings are perfectly rational. It is the dominant force behind traditional economic models, including everything you learned in school about macro- and microeconomics—thanks in no small part to its association with Adam "The Father of Economics" Smith.

Rational choice theory assumes that "agents" (economic-speak for individuals) are able to take into account all available information about a decision—probable outcomes, costs, benefits, etc.—at a moment's notice, always making the choice that maximizes their "utility" (economic-speak for benefit or personal advantage).

This perfect rationality assumption claims that irrational factors—being in a bad mood, the order in which options are presented, the skin color of the person offering you the choice, etc.—have no effect on the decision-maker.

Rational choice theory is known by a few names that you may also be familiar with, namely traditional economic theory and utility maximization theory. While there may be slight technical differences between each of these, they are fundamentally making the same argument: people are perfectly rational when making decisions.

Rational choice theory is the guiding light behind the generally accepted assumptions regarding what motivates people and why they do what they do. However, as anyone who has ever had to make a tough or split-second decision is aware, human behavior is quite a bit more complex than rational choice theory would like us to believe. As a psychology professor, Daniel Kahneman was well aware of the complexity of human behavior, but it took a unique consulting engagement for him to more fully appreciate the implications of our irrationality.

In the 1960s, Kahneman was brought in by the Israeli Air Force to teach flight instructors about the psychology of effective training. At the time, the instructors were convinced that criticism, rather than praise, was the best way to motivate their students to improve. As a psychologist, Kahneman knew that praise was in fact the better way to motivate student improvement, and, with his background in statistical analysis, he recognized that the instructors were mistaking intuition for rational analysis by attaching causal interpretations to the random fluctuations of the learning process.

As Kahneman puts it, "this was a true eureka moment."[9] His experience with the Israeli Air Force kicked off a search for other irrationalities in human thought and led to his collaboration with Tversky. Their research into cognitive biases poked definitive holes in the predictions of rational choice theory and paved the way for most of the behavioral science concepts we will discuss in this book on our journey through the sales cycle.

In his book *Arguing with Zombies,* fellow Nobel-Prize-winning economist Paul Krugman neatly summarizes what Kahneman and Tversky's work proved: "What seems terribly hard for many economists to accept is that all our models involve silly assumptions. Given what we know about cognitive psychology, utility maximization is a ludicrous concept."[10]

In reality, the decisions people make are driven by both rational factors and factors that are seemingly irrational. This fact is key to the fundamental argument made in this book: irrational factors wreak havoc throughout the sales cycle.

Unfortunately, most organizations train their salespeople to approach prospects as if they were making decisions based on pure rationality. In the process, the simple humanity of these decision-makers can be lost.

Like *"Homo economicus"*—a tongue-in-cheek reference to the perfectly logical agent of rational choice theory—most sales training methodologies assume that all decision-makers are primarily motivated to "maximize their

9   Ed Smith, "He Knew He Was Wrong—Daniel Kahneman Interview," *The Spectator*, December 12, 2011, https://www.spectator.co.uk/article/he-knew-he-was-wrong-daniel-kahneman-interview.
10   Paul Krugman, *Arguing with Zombies: Economics, Politics, and the Fight for a Better Future* (New York: W. W. Norton, 2020), p. 402.

utility," which is to say, to objectively quantify the possible outcomes of a given decision and select the one that offers the maximum value. Accordingly, decision-makers are assumed to be primarily driven by factors such as price, speed, efficiency, and so on.

However, based on insights from the various disciplines of behavioral science, we now know that nothing could be further from the truth.

In reality, prospects are just regular old people. And, like everyone else, their decision-making is heavily influenced by instinctual biases—such as preferring the status quo—which frequently leads to choices that do not provide maximum value, at least not in an objectively quantifiable sense.

It is important to note here that we do not want to attach a value, whether positive or negative, to irrationality. While some traditional economists and scientists might believe in a platonic ideal of pure reason, this is both unnecessary and impossible—it is just not the way people are wired.

No matter who you are, you are irrational at times. This is not a personality flaw; it is a part of being human. In this book, we are embracing that fact. All human thought has both rational and irrational elements. While cognitive biases present challenges, they also provide helpful impulses and information, frequently making our thought and behavior more efficient as we navigate our world.

Behavioral scientists have done remarkable work in shedding long-overdue light on these biases and other drivers that underlie human decision-making. Theirs has been an uphill battle, working against deeply entrenched and widely accepted beliefs about the rationality people are assumed to exhibit in making decisions. Only in the last few decades has their work penetrated the public consciousness and earned a critical mass of acceptance (not to mention a few Nobel Prizes).

One of the most important insights behavioral science offers is that, though they may steer people to make decisions that seem irrational, these innate biases are actually some of the most powerfully rational behaviors human beings have adapted.

Refined by the forces of natural selection over hundreds of thousands of years, these instincts increased the odds that humanity's earliest ancestors would survive and pass their genes on to the next generation. In evolutionary terms, these "irrational" biases were once some of humanity's most successful behavioral strategies.

Take overeating, for example.

Today, many in the developed world view overeating as an irrational scourge that humanity is hopelessly drawn to for no good reason. However, if we take the long view of human evolutionary history, it is actually pretty easy to understand why ancient human beings would have been rationally incentivized to eat a whole lot in one sitting:

- For the majority of the time humans have been walking around the planet, food sources were not consistent, nor were they guaranteed.
- Without reliable storage options, your own body was among the best places to store excess calories.
- As a hunter-gatherer, if you came across an abundance of edible plants or were fortunate enough to hunt and kill a large animal, you

would have been wise to get while the getting was good—before someone else came along to challenge you for the bounty.

- Taking advantage of excess supplies of calories would improve your health relative to those who were less calorie-fortunate, which would increase your odds of survival which would increase your odds of passing on your genes—which, per evolutionary logic, is an optimal outcome.

To state the obvious, the world today is much different than it was back then. Our modern, post-Agricultural-Revolution reality—which has only lasted for the blink of an eye in our long view of human history—is a radical departure from the daily life-and-death struggle that our hunter-gatherer ancestors experienced on the savannas of eastern Africa.

- For the entire time you and I have been walking around the planet, especially if we are walking around in the more developed parts of the world, our food sources have likely been abundant.
- We benefit from the modern miracles of electricity and cold storage, which extend the shelf life of any and all calories we might need later on, and we no longer have reason to hoard excess calories within our bodies.
- Yet overeating persists to the point that there are more obese people than there are starving people in the world today, and medical complications directly related to obesity rank among humanity's top killers.[11]

---

11   "More Obese People in the World Than Underweight, Says Study," BBC, April 1, 2016.

If we were *Homo economicus*—perfectly rational and optimally adapted to our present circumstances—overeating would be much less common in today's world.

Why hasn't our behavior adapted to this new food-abundant reality?

Simply put, this new version of reality came upon humanity too quickly for our survival instincts to adapt. When the world goes through a radical change in a relatively short period of time—such as the proliferation of plant and animal domestication which gave birth to our current food-abundant reality sometime around twelve thousand years ago—human beings can't catch up. We continue behaving in the same instinctual ways as though nothing has changed.

Instinctual behavioral adaption takes a *long* time. It took hundreds of thousands of years for evolution to slowly shift our eating patterns. The last twelve thousand or so post-agricultural-revolution years just has not been enough time for our instincts and biological urges to adjust to our current food-abundant reality.

Not surprisingly, overeating is not the only human behavior that can be understood through this lens.

GHOSTS IN THE MACHINE

*"...the great innovators in the history of science
had always been aware of the transparency of
phenomena toward a different order of reality, of
the ubiquitous presence of the
ghost in the machine..."*
—Arthur Koestler[12]

12   "Ghost in the machine" is a phrase coined by British philosopher Gilbert Ryle in his description of René Descartes' mind-body dualism, which claims

For a long time, the convention in the scientific world was that human brains evolved strictly to process factual information about their environment. However, it is now hypothesized that this is far from the entirety of the picture. I would like to introduce you to a compelling theory that more accurately accounts for the well-documented biases that haunt human decision-making.

The *social brain hypothesis*, proposed by British anthropologist Robin Dunbar, argues that human intelligence did not evolve primarily as a means to solve the increasingly complex problems presented by the physical environment that surrounded our ancestors, but rather as a means of surviving and reproducing in large and complex social groups.[13]

When grouped together with an idea known as the *updated savanna hypothesis,*[14] the two comprise what William von Hippel calls the *social leap* in his book of the same name.[15]

Here is a quick summary of what you need to know about the updated savanna hypothesis:

- Tectonic activity millions of years ago gradually replaced our ancestors' rainforest home with open savanna.

that mental and physical activity occur simultaneously but separately. Ryle introduced the phrase in *The Concept of Mind* (1949). Arthur Koestler brought the concept to wider attention in his 1967 book *The Ghost in the Machine*. According to Koestler, the human brain has primitive brain structures—the "ghost in the machine"—that can overpower higher, more developed functions. See Gilbert Ryle, *The Concept of Mind* (Chicago: University of Chicago Press, 1949); Arthur Koestler, *The Ghost in the Machine* (New York: Macmillan, 1967).

13   Robin I. M. Dunbar, "The Social Brain Hypothesis," *Evolutionary Anthropology* 6, no. 5 (December 1998): 178–90.

14   The savanna hypothesis originally proposed by Ray Dart in 1925—based on his discovery of Australopithecus africanus, or "the man-ape of South Africa"—argued that migration into the open savannas was a fundamental driver of our ancestors' evolution, but did not explain what caused said migration. The savanna hypothesis has since been updated to incorporate our contemporary understanding of tectonic plate movement as the cause of climate change in the East African Rift Valley that drove our ancestors from the forest to the savanna.

15   William von Hippel, *The Social Leap: The New Evolutionary Science of Who We Are, Where We Come From, and What Makes Us Happy* (New York: HarperCollins, 2018).

- In the savanna, we were easy prey, prompting our ancestors to huddle and cluster more closely together than tree-dwelling chimps for safety's sake.
- Their adaptation to this lifestyle included becoming more social and cooperative, traits which were evolutionarily advantageous in a group.
- The greatest challenge to cooperation as a community survival technique is free-riding: individuals skipping the hard work while sharing the benefits of the community.
- In this environment, fairness became a moral precept.
- The threat of ostracization became the greatest stick our ancestors had in enforcing cooperation.

The social brain hypothesis suggests that primates evolved large brains in order to manage the social challenges brought about by this newfound cooperation. In particular, our ancestors developed larger brains as they began to share information with one another, making for a more effective and productive group where, rather than each individual learning solely through trial and error, everyone could build on each other's achievements.

This is the social leap.

The dynamic duo of the updated savanna hypothesis plus the social brain hypothesis—aka the social leap—forms the foundation of many of this book's arguments. Over the course of thousands of generations, our ancestors developed instinctual biases and mental shortcuts that enabled them to get along in their social world more effectively and efficiently. Fast-forward to the present, and these biases and shortcuts represent an important part of our cognitive inheritance.

Unfortunately, much of what served us so well in prehistoric, pre-industrialized society is mismatched to our present circumstances.

Today, these formerly rational biases constitute systemic glitches in our mental machinery. This is true of everyone—you and your prospects and customers included. **No matter how rational people try to be, and no matter how hard they try to optimize their decision-making, their thinking is unavoidably haunted by these glitches.**

These glitches are ghosts in the machine.

The *machine* is our awe-inspiring mental capability, inherited from our evolutionary past, which enables our unmatched decision-making abilities. The *ghosts* are the biases we have also inherited from our evolutionary past, which often present themselves in our modern world as deviations from rational decision-making.

Ghosts in the Machine is a systematic approach to managing and overcoming a certain set of biases that have the greatest impact on decision-making in the specific context of the sales cycle.

WE'VE COME A LONG WAY, BABY

> *"You don't have to reinvent the wheel,*
> *just attach it to a new wagon."*
> —*Mark McCormack*

In the late 1800s, America's migration west was in full bloom. People were drawn from the east to the west—made newly accessible to the masses with the expansion of the railroad system—by the discovery of gold and silver, as well as the promise of adventure, opportunity, and free land.

Far less developed than the eastern parts of the US and lacking in the type of retail infrastructure that would provide life's necessities and conveniences, the west presented fertile ground for a new breed of professional: the traveling salesman.

Traveling from town to town selling their goods, often directly out of the covered wagon they arrived in, these salespeople earned a nefarious reputation for making outlandish and unfounded claims about the miraculous benefits of their wares. Further, it was not uncommon for these salespeople to secretly pay individuals to enmesh themselves in a crowd of potential customers and sing the praises of whatever was on offer in order to juice interest and convince others to make a purchase. These salespeople became infamously known as "snake oil" salesmen and are largely responsible for the tainted opinion that still dogs the sales profession today.

In 1886, against this backdrop, John H. Patterson, president of National Cash Register (NCR), developed a new way to sell goods to potential customers. Known as Pyramid Selling, Patterson's method was arguably the first formal and codified professional selling system. At its core, the method called on salespeople to sell NCR's cash registers to the most influential businessmen in a town by focusing their pitch on how the machine would help solve problems, rather than simply boasting of its amazing features.

Patterson's influence on the sales profession persists to this day. One of his former sales managers, Thomas J. Watson, adopted the principles of Pyramid Selling in the launch of International Business Machines, better known today as IBM. Much of IBM's success through the years can be directly tied to Watson's embrace of Patterson's professional approach to selling.

Although Pyramid Selling in its original form is no longer in use, Patterson's approach has evolved and grown and continues to be a broadly used and successful approach for selling to prospects, in particular as the foundation of Solution Selling.

The sales profession has come a long way from its snake oil roots in the late 1800s.

Today, the blocking and tackling of succeeding as a salesperson is well-worn ground. If you have read a sales book prior to this one, or been through a sales training program or seminar, the material was most likely based on a specific sales methodology. In no particular order, here are some of the most popular sales methods in practice today:

- **Solution Selling**—This method focuses on solving problems, not on the product or service.
- **Value-Based Selling**—This method focuses on the value of your product or service, not the product or service itself.
- **Consultative Selling**—This method focuses on becoming a trusted advisor to the prospect or customer. (CustomerCentric Selling® and the Sandler Selling Method are cousins to this method)
- **SPIN®-Selling**—In 1988, Neil Rackham created this method, which focuses on asking the right *situation, problem, implication,* and *need-payoff* questions.

- **The Challenger Sale**—Matthew Dixon and Brent Adamson introduced this method in 2011, claiming that "challengers" use the *teach-tailor-take* method to close a deal.
- **SNAP Selling**—Introduced by Jill Konrath in 2012, this method focuses on being *simple, invaluable, aligned with the needs of the customer,* and a *priority.*

Though varying in approach, these methodologies—along with many more that have not been included here—have withstood the test of time and proven, when applied faithfully, to be effective systems for converting prospects into customers. These systems are sales mousetraps that work.

Ghosts in the Machine is *not* another sales mousetrap.

The guidance in the following pages is not meant to replace these proven methodologies. **Rather, the material presented here is meant to be complementary to all sales methodologies.** If embraced and applied, the novel insights I will share with you in this book will help salespeople achieve more success in leveraging whichever methodology they subscribe to as their foundational go-to-market strategy.

VIEWING THE SALES CYCLE THROUGH THE LENS OF BEHAVIORAL SCIENCE

> *"If I have seen further it is by standing on the shoulders of giants."*
> —Sir Isaac Newton

In our exploration of human biases and decision-making glitches, we stand on the shoulders of giants.

Much of what you will find in this volume has been taken from work done by the greatest minds known to behavioral science. Robin Dunbar, William von Hippel, Daniel Kahneman, Amos Tversky, Richard Thaler, Carol Dweck, Robert Cialdini, and many others like them have done most of the heavy lifting to reveal how and why these behavioral ghosts influence human thinking—and how to mitigate their glitchy effects.

While a wide variety of biases have been cataloged by behavioral scientists through the years, many of them will not be found here. This is not to say that those neglected biases are unimportant; however, they are less impactful in the specific context of the sales cycle, and so I have chosen to focus our limited time elsewhere.

We will instead home in on the behavioral science insights that most impact the sales cycle and organize them into an actionable system that will positively impact your business-development efforts. This system is designed to work in tandem with your chosen sales methodology.

This book is chock-full of advice that is applicable to your life as a salesperson, regardless of the products or services you represent. The advice in this book is also broadly applicable to all types of selling situations—from retail to business sales—and all types of customers—from individual consumers to C-suite executives. However, the guidance herein is most applicable to the following types of sales:

- **Business-to-business**—the sale of products and services from one business to another, as opposed to sales to individual consumers or government organizations
- **Complex sales**—sales cycles that have long execution timelines, multiple competitors, large

contract values, and multiple stakeholders, as opposed to transactional sales like stock trading or office supplies

- **C-suite sales**—sales to an executive with a *C* in their job title (CEO, CFO, COO, etc.) who is the ultimate signing authority
- **Recurring business**—a selling environment that requires an ongoing, long-term relationship between the seller and the buyer

If your selling circumstances require a certain level of personal, ongoing service to senior-level executives at for-profit companies, and a long execution or implementation cycle,[16] the advice and recommendations in this book are squarely in your wheelhouse.

That said, however, the vast majority of what we will be discussing in the following pages will be valuable and helpful regardless of your specific selling circumstances. Much of that value comes from filling in the gaps in traditional sales training.

Most sales methodologies fall short of being maximally effective for one of two reasons:

1. **They rely on a purely rational approach to decision-making and the sales cycle.**
2. **They are too narrowly focused on one subset of the sales cycle.**

The first set of methodologies presents clearly defined structures that paint a picture of how the sales cycle *should* unfold, but these methodologies lack appreciation for how behavioral biases influence decision-making, and therefore

---

16   Examples of this type of selling include, but are not limited to, banking and financial services, SaaS and technology services, consulting and professional service sales.

limit their own effectiveness. Each of the methodologies listed above falls into this category.

The second set of methodologies, though they may provide valuable insights for a specific stage in the sales cycle, do not offer guidance on how to approach sales from start to finish, requiring salespeople to look elsewhere for help. Classic examples are books solely focused on prospecting—such as Jeb Blount's *Fanatical Prospecting*—or negotiating—such as Roger Fisher and William Ury's *Getting to Yes*.

Again, *Ghosts in the Machine* is not intended to replace your preferred sales methodology, but to enhance its effectiveness while addressing some of these deficiencies.

To do that, this book will decode the full sales cycle through the prism of behavioral science, guiding you toward an understanding of the irrational ghosts in the machine that resist rational sales efforts, all while unlocking new insights that you can use to great benefit wherever you are in the sales cycle.

THE SALES JOURNEY

> *"Sales is an outcome, not a goal. It's a function of doing numerous things right, starting from the moment you target a potential prospect until you finalize the deal."*
> —Jill Konrath

In general, the sales cycle is composed of five stages:[17]

17 *Of course* this is not the only way to break down the sales cycle. Many people argue that the sales cycle really begins with market research to identify leads or suspects, which comes before prospecting. Others argue that the sales cycle needs to include stages specifically for presenting and handling objections. Others still argue that the sales cycle ends with closing or follow-up

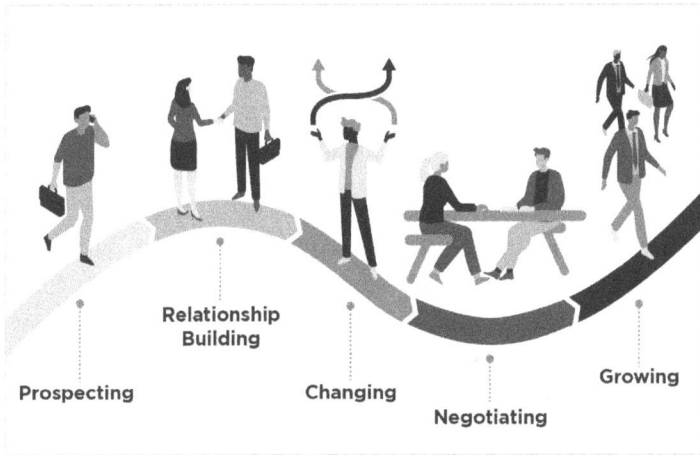

Accordingly, we will work through the sales cycle using these five stages as our structural guide, introducing you to the ghosts you are likely to encounter along the way and offering strategies to effectively manage them.

For purposes of simplicity, these stages are presented sequentially. On our journey through the sales cycle we will go through prospecting before moving into relationship building, and we will go through relationship building before we move into changing, and so on. Although during your career you will experience exceptions to this linear presentation—such as being thrust into a negotiation in support of a sales team at the last minute, or being referred into an account and never needing to prospect your way in—these stages most often unfold in order.

Some salespeople are not responsible for every stage of the sales cycle. For example, oftentimes, inside salespeople are specifically responsible for prospecting and setting

---

stages. In my opinion, these are semantic arguments that lose sight of the forest for the trees. The approach presented here covers the vast majority of sales bases, even if some would argue that I haven't defined the stages "correctly."

initial appointments, passing responsibility for the remaining stages of the sales cycle on to someone else. Or, on the other end of the spectrum, some salespeople are only engaged once an initial deal has been closed and take responsibility for growing the share of wallet with a given customer.

If your circumstances dictate that only some of the stages within the full sales cycle apply to you, feel free to focus your time on just those stages in this book. That said, whatever your specific selling circumstances, having an appreciation for all the stages will only enhance your abilities at any given point, and during your sales career there is a high likelihood you will eventually interact with other stages at some point even if you are not currently doing so.

Finally, as you make your way through this book, keep in mind that there are no set expectations regarding the timing of the stages of the sales cycle. Some relationships will click instantly, while others will take years. Some sales cycles are quick and painless, while others seem to drag on forever. For the purposes of this book, do not worry about the specific timing of any given stage. Let go of concern for how long it takes for a new relationship to take root. Focus on the process of getting to know your prospects, the process of understanding the ghosts that haunt their mental machinery. The timing, which will be unique for each relationship, will take care of itself.

PROSPECTING

The prospecting stage may be viewed as the prologue to the sales cycle.

By definition, a prologue is "an event or action that leads to another event or situation." In this case, prospecting is the action that provides entry into the sales cycle. Before we can do any selling, we have to find people to sell to. At the beginning of our journey through the sales cycle, we will learn that in order to find enough people to sell to, the most important thing we need to do is get out of our own way.

In Prospecting we will be introduced to the deceitful ghosts in the machine, which make finding prospects even harder than it already is. These ghosts cripple our own prospecting efforts, enabling the classic excuses most salespeople are all too familiar with.

By leveraging insights from behavioral science, we will come to understand why salespeople are their own worst enemy when playing the numbers game that sits at the heart of the prospecting stage of the sales cycle. Then we will focus our efforts on creating a smart process to circumvent the effects of these deceitful ghosts.

RELATIONSHIP BUILDING

We must not put the selling cart before the relationship horse.

Relationship building *must* take priority over pitching in the initial stages of the sales cycle. Before we can have sustainable success selling our wares, we have to connect with the human being we hope to sell to. The ability to form a bond with our prospects begins—just as it does in our social relationships—with liking.

In Relationship Building, we will be confronted with the lazy ghosts in the machine that motivate prospects and customers to take the path of least resistance and filter new information through pre-established beliefs which

typically frame salespeople as antagonists. As we pull the curtain back on this inherent laziness, we will reveal some of the most foundational behavioral science concepts and come away with a deeper appreciation for the irrational workings of the human mind.

Rather than push back against the resistance created by the lazy ghosts, we will use insights from behavioral science to better connect with them and move from being an antagonist to being liked. Hint: it begins with listening.

CHANGING

Selling is about affecting change. And changing is arguably the most challenging stage of the sales cycle.

At the risk of stating the obvious, before a decision-maker chooses to make a change, they have to think about it. Unfortunately, too many salespeople disregard *how* their prospects think about making a change, falsely assuming that their pitch needs be focused on all the rational reasons a decision-maker should make a change.

In Changing we will meet the busy and fearful ghosts that loom large when prospects consider a change, feeding on their limited attention and fear of uncertainty and encouraging them to decide not to decide. In an effort to better understand why making a change is so daunting, we will dive even deeper into the evolution of thought and gain a better appreciation for the allure of the status quo, the salesperson's fiercest competitor.

We will use critical insights from behavioral science to learn to mitigate the influence of these pesky ghosts by using storytelling to frame rational reasons in a way that prospects will relate to and remember. In addition, we will double down on the importance of listening as a means to prime those ideas our prospects care most about.

NEGOTIATING

Human beings are just as cooperative as they are competitive.

At this point in the sales cycle, our prospect has decided to make a change, and now we must negotiate the details of our future partnership, formally sealing the deal. Contrary to the "your win is my loss" perception most people naturally have, replicable success in negotiating comes from collaborating with your counterparty, not competing with them. Applying this insight is critical in better recognizing the game we are playing when we sit down at the negotiating table.

In Negotiating, we will see how the competitive and stubborn ghosts in the machine wire salespeople to view the world in terms of scarcity and rigidity—which is exactly how we *do not* want to act if we hope to be successful in our negotiations. Negotiating is not about winning. Instead, we need to partner with our prospects to expand the pie, be flexible, and look for more optimal solutions.

Embracing cooperation when we are negotiating helps disarm the ghosts that pull both us and our prospects away from more optimal outcomes. Behavioral science teaches us that focusing on interests, not positions, is the key to a successful negotiation. That, and being prepared.

GROWING

Growth comes via the embrace of transformation.

To be successful, a sales function and its salespeople must grow. But, paradoxically, growing—both personally and professionally—is something that most salespeople (and people in general) struggle with.

In Growing, we will explore the self-centered ghosts in the machine that lead salespeople to disregard perspectives outside of their own, unnecessarily limiting their personal growth and development. Further, this self-centered approach makes us overly optimistic, holding us back from taking advantage of the one thing that would have the greatest impact on our professional growth: referrals. And we will see why being self-centered is a weakness disguised as a strength.

At the end of our sales journey, we will leverage behavioral science to challenge these ghosts that keep us too focused on ourselves and too optimistic. In doing so, we will open ourselves up to a mindset that embraces transformation, while also making a commitment to seeking out the help we need the most.

TIPPING THE SCALES

> *"May the odds be ever in your favor."*
> *—Effie Trinket, from The Hunger Games by*
> *Suzanne Collins*

The approach to the sales cycle presented in this book is firmly rooted in a behavioral science perspective because behavioral science is applicable to the vast majority of situations you will find yourself in when engaging a prospect or customer. Using this approach will help you become more efficient and effective in every stage of the sales cycle, from prospecting to closing to growing your business.

However, there is no promise of instant results. If you are looking for the ability to magically eliminate the resistance you experience throughout the sales cycle, you have come to the wrong place. There is no quick fix for these ghosts. Understanding and appreciating the ghosts in the machine will not give you the power to bend people to your will.

Our goal in understanding and appreciating the ghosts in the machine is not to eliminate them. These ghosts have been around long before us, and they will last long after we are gone. Just as twelve thousand years has been unable to loosen the grip of humanity's overeating instincts, our most diligent and sincere efforts will not clear our prospects of the biases that cause them to resist our sales efforts.

Rather, our primary goal is to be aware of these ghosts. Awareness, as we will see throughout our sales journey, is one of the most powerful tools we have to manage the resistance we encounter. And changing how we approach these situations will not happen overnight; it will take time and focused effort.

Fortunately, these ghosts are not shy. When the spotlight hits them, they proudly and predictably demonstrate their effects. Their predictability offers us the unique opportunity to learn what to expect from them and respond accordingly. That is the opportunity you will find in this book.

Once you understand and appreciate the ghosts in the machine that have the greatest impact on decision-making, you will be able to consistently tip the scales in your favor, enabling you to efficiently and effectively uncover

new opportunities, establish and build better relationships, affect change, negotiate better deals, and create a sustainable sales growth engine.

I hope you are as excited to see where this journey will lead as I am to guide you through it.

———

P.S. One more thing before we jump in.

If I am able to deliver on the promise outlined in this introduction—if at least a few of the following insights resonate with you and you plan to leverage them in your sales journey—will you commit to going to my website, *www.RyanVoeltz.com*, and joining my email distribution list?

Deal?

Okay. Let's get started!

PROSPECTING

Ted Williams, Baseball Hall of Famer, lifetime .344 batter,[18] and one of the greatest hitters to ever play the game, once said, "Baseball is the only field of endeavor where a man can succeed three times out of ten and be considered a good performer."

With all due respect, I doubt that "Teddy Baseball" ever tried his hand at sales prospecting.

Contacting and engaging a prospect in a meaningful dialogue is a humbling exercise with a very low probability of success. According to Salesforce,[19] telephone prospecting has a meager 8.21% conversion rate. Email prospecting is even more dismal, with a paltry 0.03% conversion rate.

---

18   For those unfamiliar, a .344 batting average translates to a hit per every 3.44 out of 10 times at bat.

19   Stuart Leung, "You Never Call Anymore: The Case for Sales Phone Calls Over Email," *Salesforce Blog*, February 12, 2014, https://www.salesforce.com/content/blogs/us/en/2014/02/email-vs-phone-calls-business.html.

Prospecting is not for the faint of heart. In fact, 40% of salespeople say that prospecting is the most challenging part of the sales process.[20]

In terms of challenges presented versus successes achieved, hitting a baseball has nothing on sales prospecting. For a salesperson, getting prospects to respond three times out of ten would be nothing short of a miracle.

No matter your strategy or approach, no matter how knowledgeable or experienced you may be, you will fail to connect with prospects far more often than you will succeed. And you will have no choice but to keep banging away for the long haul. There is no light at the of the tunnel where prospecting gets any easier. If you have not done so already, you would do well to embrace this fact of professional selling now.

Prospecting is a numbers game, and, like it or not, low response rates are just the name of the game.

PLAYING THE NUMBERS GAME

Although there are various reasons prospects respond with such low frequency, the primary reason prospecting has such a low probability of success is that you often need to be in the right place at the right time in order to succeed. Per a survey by the RAIN Group, 75% of decision-makers responded that the biggest factor determining whether they would respond to an inbound sales call was whether or not they had a current need for a product or service.[21]

---

20 "130 Eye-Opening Sales Statistics for 2021 (by Category)," Spotio, October 21, 2020, https://spotio.com/blog/sales-statistics/.

21 Mike Schultz, Jason Murray, and Gord Smith, *5 Sales Prospecting Myths Debunked: 488 Buyers Sound Off about How Sellers Get Through and Win Their Business*, RAIN Group Center for Sales Research, https://www.rainsalestraining.com/resources/sales-white-papers/5-sales-prospecting-myths-debunked

Unfortunately, prior to engaging in a dialogue, a salesperson has no way of knowing what a prospect's current product or service needs are. In other words, a given prospect's receptivity to a given value prop is out of the salesperson's control.

Fortunately, what *is* in the salesperson's control is the number of prospects they call on, which is the best way to increase the odds of being in the right place at the right time. **Playing the numbers game well is the cornerstone of a successful sales career and the most important part[22] of the prospecting stage of the sales cycle.**

The goal here is *not* to detail the specifics of a comprehensive prospecting strategy; there are a variety of other guides[23] out there that are purely focused on prospecting if that is what you are looking for. Rather, in the spirit of the Pareto Principle—more commonly known as the 80/20 rule—we will hereby focus on the one single aspect of prospecting that, more than any other, determines the difference between success and failure: doing a sufficient volume of prospecting.

I went through my first formal sales training program with Lanier-Ricoh way back in 2001. One of the few things I recall with any detail from the weeklong program is the classic image of a sales funnel, separated by horizontal layers from top to bottom. While there are a few different versions of

---

22   One could argue that targeting is as important as volume simply because in order of operations it comes first, and if you spend all day calling the wrong people you are not going to get anywhere. This is a valid argument, but, for purposes of this book, I am assuming you have got the wherewithal to find the right prospects without my help.

23   A few of the most popular are Jeb Blount, *Fanatical Prospecting: The Ultimate Guide for Starting Sales Conversations and Filling the Pipeline by Leveraging Social Selling, Telephone, E-mail, and Cold Calling* (Hoboken, NJ: Wiley, 2015); Marylou Tyler and Jeremey Donovan, *Predictable Prospecting: How to Radically Increase Your B2B Sales Pipeline* (New York: McGraw-Hill, 2016); and Mike Weinberg, *New Sales. Simplified.* (New York: AMACOM, 2012).

the sales funnel, they all generally conform to the same layout: the top layer—the widest layer—represents the prospecting stage of the sales process, the middle layers represent various intermediate stages of the sales process, and the bottom layer—the narrowest layer—represents the conversion of a prospect into a paying customer.

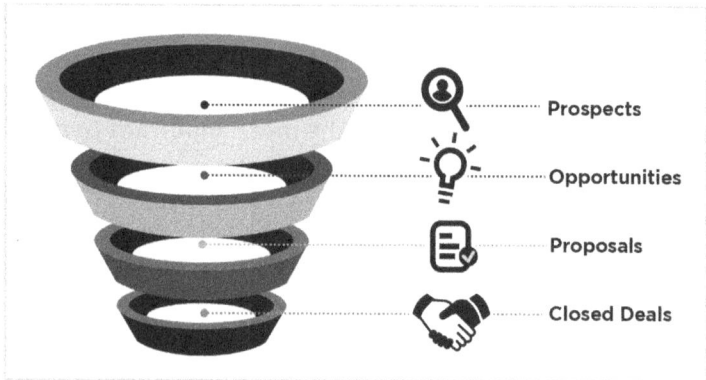

The image simply communicates that you need to have a lot of prospects[24] enter the top of your funnel if you want to have enough paying customers come out the other end. The sales funnel succinctly and accurately illustrates the numbers game dynamic, and it looks essentially the same today as it did in 2001—and in 1981—and in 1961.

Here is the problem: salespeople do not embrace and leverage this fundamental concept to their advantage.

My experience over two decades of working as a professional salesperson, with and around other professional salespeople, has proven this time and time again. Despite its simplicity and obviousness, many salespeople seem to

---

24   Or "leads," which many sales program differentiate as the formal classification of a company when it first enters your sales funnel, with leads moving down into the "prospects" layer of the sales funnel only after a pre-determined level of connection with the company has been made.

go out of their way to avoid properly filling the top layer of their sales funnel with prospects, and as a result, they end up reaping a meager output of customers from the bottom layer.

The most common mistake salespeople make when prospecting—the thing that keeps them from filling their funnel—is a lack of sufficient call volume. The data supports these observations.

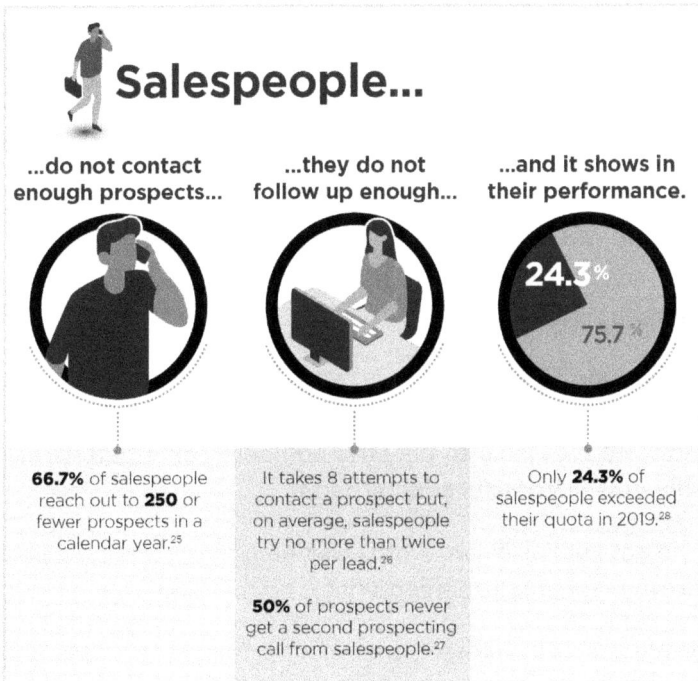

Salespeople...

...do not contact enough prospects...	...they do not follow up enough...	...and it shows in their performance.
66.7% of salespeople reach out to **250** or fewer prospects in a calendar year.[25]	It takes 8 attempts to contact a prospect but, on average, salespeople try no more than twice per lead.[26] **50%** of prospects never get a second prospecting call from salespeople.[27]	Only **24.3%** of salespeople exceeded their quota in 2019.[28]

24.3%

75.7%

25   Marc Wayshak, "18 New Sales Statistics for 2020 from Our Groundbreaking Study!," Sales Insights Lab, March 12, 2020, https://salesinsightslab.com/sales-research/.

26   Per Telenet and Ovation Sales Group.

27   Per Velocify.

28   Wayshak, "Sales Statistics for 2020."

More than anything else, prospecting provides the foundation which will determine how much success a salesperson or organization will achieve. Excel at prospecting, and you will succeed in spite of other shortcomings you may have. Underperform in your prospecting efforts, and your long-term success in sales will be unavoidably stunted, no matter how great you are at everything else.

I find it telling that sales organizations will often tolerate salespeople who are selfish, abrasive, difficult to work with, lacking in punctuality, inconsistent in reporting, and on and on—simply because they consistently uncover new opportunities with their prospecting efforts. This lenience showcases how much sales organizations value those who are consistently successful at prospecting.

Finding new customers is the lifeblood of any business, and, tragically, there are relatively few people who consistently do it well.

What, specifically, do those who are able to consistently keep their funnels full do to maintain sufficient call volume? How are they able to play the numbers game better than their less-successful counterparts?

The answer lies in two words that are known to send a chill down many a salesperson's back: cold calling.

There are two types of prospecting calls: warm calls and cold calls. Both are critical to your success as a salesperson, but only one may be relied on as the foundation for sustained success throughout a sales career.

- A *warm call* is one in which an introduction is made for you via a referral, or one where no introduction is needed thanks to a pre-established relationship you already have with the prospect.

- Warm calling is the easier form of prospecting, which we will revisit at the end of our journey when we discuss growing your business.
- **A *cold call* is one in which you try to make a connection with a company without the benefit of a pre-existing relationship.**
  - Cold calling is a different beast entirely. It is a Sisyphean task in which just trying to get your foot in the door can take a gargantuan effort.

In an effort to provide you with as much value as possible and help you build a foundation for success that you can rely on, we are going to focus our time here on cold calling.

To be clear, when I refer to cold calling in this book, I mean picking up the telephone, dialing a phone number, and trying to have a conversation with a prospect. While salespeople should prospect and cold call using every method available—calling, emailing, social media messaging, visiting in person, etc.—the good old phone call is still the golden standard when it comes to maximizing the likelihood that we will make an initial connection with our prospects.

There are four specific reasons why phone calls stand out in a world gone email-crazy:

Executives...

...are swamped by email...	...and likely will not open yours.	Executives prefer a phone call...	...and phone calls just perform better.
A typical businessperson receives more than **115** emails every day.[29]	In the U.S., an average of only **23.1%** of emails are opened.[30]	**57%** of C-level buyers prefer that salespeople call them.[31]	Phone calls to prospects out-convert email outreach **8.21%** to 0.031%.[32]

Again, you will certainly need to leverage other methods of contacting and communicating with your prospects, and emailing is likely option 1B to calling's 1A. My point in stressing the use of actual phone calls is twofold: one, they have become a lost art with our collective obsession with email; and two, they are simply the most effective prospecting tool available.

29   Sara Radicati, ed., *Email Statistics Report, 2011–2015*, Radicati Group, https://www.radicati.com/wp/wp-content/uploads/2011/05/Email-Statistics-Report-2011-2015-Executive-Summary.pdf

30   IBM Watson Marketing, *2018 Marketing Benchmark Report: Email and Mobile Metrics for Smarter Marketing*, May 2018, https://advance.biz-tech-insights.com/whitepaper/Watson-Marketing-Digital-Benchmark-Report.pdf

31   Schultz, Murray, and Smith, *Prospecting Myths Debunked*.

32   Leung, "You Never Call Anymore."

PROSPECTING IS HARD ENOUGH.
SALESPEOPLE MAKE IT HARDER.

"You can have results or excuses, not both."
—Anonymous

In business, growth is priority number one. Other priorities will come and go, but growth will always be at the top of the list for businesses interested in their own longevity. The sales function exists as the primary means for a company to execute their growth plans. And the most effective way for the sales function to drive growth for the overall company is by finding and contacting new prospects and converting them into paying customers.

Yet, despite all the evidence to point toward this fact, many salespeople would rather be doing anything but prospecting and cold calling. Too many salespeople talk themselves out of the clear and primary importance of prospecting volume, limiting their ability to perform and inevitably making a brutally challenging numbers game even harder.

Rather than addressing the eight-hundred-pound numbers game elephant in the room, many salespeople allow the innate difficulty of cold calling to seduce them into trying alternative strategies. Because these misguided attempts to circumvent the cold, hard reality of the prospecting numbers game generally cluster around a handful of ubiquitous excuses, I now offer a few gentle counterpoints to challenge the flawed logic behind these well-meaning but ineffective strategies.

- **Excuse: Prospects will call me when they have a need.**
  - How will they know to call you if you have never or rarely called them?

- Between you and another competitor who *has* been calling, why would they call you? Would *you* call you?
- **Excuse: I need more information before I call.**
  - Cold calling by its very nature means that there will be significant gaps in your knowledge prior to calling; because you have no pre-established relationship with the prospect, you will always feel like you could use more information.
  - Better to call once you have acquired a *minimum* threshold of information and learn the rest straight from the horse's mouth.
- **Excuse: I will call later, when a better prospect list is created.**
  - No prospect list has ever been or will ever be perfect.
  - A list is just a map of your sales territory; it is intended to guide you. Just like actual maps, lists are not and do not need to be a perfect reflection of reality; they need to be good enough to get you from *A* to *B*, no more.
- **Excuse: It is my partner's responsibility to bring me leads.**
  - You are responsible for your sales success—or failure.
  - Are you comfortable allowing someone else to determine how well you will do?
- **Excuse: I need to take care of some other stuff—administrative work, current account management, dealing with internal company politics—before I start prospecting.**
  - These things on their own are important, but none of them will help you build a pipeline

of new opportunities, nor will they enable sustained business growth.

- There is only so much time in each day, and time spent focusing on other things is time not spent on prospecting for new business.

If you recognize these distracting tactics, or others like them, either in yourself or in others—I know I still see them in myself—then you are familiar with the self-deceit that derails the best intentions of so many prospecting salespeople.

Why is it so easy for so many of us to fall into these excuses of self-deceit?

Fortunately, the lens of behavioral science offers us some very clear reasons. As it turns out, prospecting is an activity that swims against a mental current powered by a few key cognitive biases innate to the human mind.

Evolution has left the human brain some major hurdles to get over when it comes to calling an exhaustive list of strangers on the phone. And while we cannot change brain behavior that evolved over millions of years overnight, it is within our control to learn about the evolutionary biases that affect prospecting success and, crucially, change our attitude toward these ghosts, empowering us to dodge their deceitful influence.

To understand how to overcome our difficulties with prospecting, we need to understand how our minds think about prospecting. While most of this book will be focused on the ghosts in the machine that haunt the minds of prospects and customers, we will begin our journey by drawing attention to those ghosts that have the greatest impact on *the salesperson's* decision-making.

DECEIVING OURSELVES

"Man is his own worst enemy."
—Cicero

Let's face it: the first and most difficult challenge we are up against during the prospecting stage of sales is not the resistance of our customers. It is our own resistance to the task of calling up and connecting with a sufficient number of strangers. Thanks to the deceitful ghosts in the machine, when it comes to prospecting, we really are our own worst enemy.

Fear not. Being your own worst enemy is nothing to be ashamed of. In fact, you are in good company. Evolution has programmed every human being on the planet to struggle with the ghosts in the machine in a wide variety of ways. Fortunately for you, there are just a few key ghosts that do most of the haunting when it comes to prospecting.

If we look back on them, the excuses I outlined above can be grouped into three primary categories of self-deceit that haunt prospecting salespeople:

- **Being afraid that people will not like you.**
  - An aversion to being turned down often makes salespeople reluctant to pick up the phone.
  - This is one of humanity's strongest and most universal fears, underlying most excuses for not calling enough prospects.
- **Believing that you are somehow different than everyone else.**
  - Assuming that people will call you and that your partners will do the heavy lifting, therefore granting you special dispensation not to

put effort into prospecting, falls under this umbrella.

- This is what lies underneath the idea that the numbers game does not apply to you.
- **Seeking instant gratification.**
  - Instead of the stress of cold calls, salespeople look for something that can be finished easily and give them a sense of satisfaction. Wanting more information, waiting for a better list, and doing everything else instead of prospecting can all be traced back to this root.
  - This is why salespeople put off prospecting's heavy lifting until sometime later.

These three categories of deception are promoted, respectively, by the ghosts of *fear of rejection*, *false uniqueness*, and *procrastination*. Together, this trio comprises the deceitful ghosts—the major root causes of prospecting underperformance.

FEAR OF REJECTION

To fear rejection is to fear that other people will not embrace you. When you hear your inner voice asking "What if they say no?" you are hearing the ghost of the fear of rejection.

As far as we know, fear of rejection is a universal human condition. While it manifests within people to different degrees, with some feeling it more acutely than others, there is little doubt that we all experience this emotion. Take public speaking, for example. A survey by researchers at Chapman University found that a fear of public speaking is a significant phobia among Americans. Almost a third of all respondents said they feared speaking in front of a crowd, a higher percentage than those who were afraid of muggings, snakes, needles, or flying.[33]

Strip the fear of public speaking down to its core and what you will find is a simple fear that the crowd will reject you.

In the evolutionary terms of the social leap hypothesis we discussed in the introduction, the fear of rejection can be attributed to the fear of being ostracized from the group. Millions of years ago, being ostracized from the group was effectively a death sentence. Outside of the safety and protection of the group, our ancient ancestors, alone on the savanna, would have been unable to fend off large predators, and the expected life span of any individual who was ostracized would have been significantly shortened.

Although we live radically different lives today than our ancestors did back then, and literal life-and-death situations have become comparatively rare, each of us still carries and uses the same primal machinery, which is constantly on alert for signs that we may be ostracized from the group. Our evolution toward cooperation—our social leap—had the unintended consequence of giving birth to the ghost of fear of rejection, the fear that we might be cut off from essential cooperation.

In some sense, salespeople spend a significant portion of their professional lives voluntarily being rejected.

Salespeople will hear *no* way more than they will hear *yes*. This is a cold, hard fact; we need look for no further evidence than the remarkably low cold-calling conversion rates we discussed earlier. **But to hear *no* all day long is to constantly trigger the fear of rejection ghost, which can**

33   Shreya Sheth, *America's Top Fears 2019*, Chapman University, 2019, https://www.chapman.edu/wilkinson/research-centers/babbie-center/_files/americas-top-fears-2019.pdf

cause upsetting and persistent emotional reactions, and often does its best to convince the salesperson that prospecting is just not worth the heartache.

FALSE UNIQUENESS

False uniqueness is a bias toward perceiving yourself as above average, especially in terms of flattering or desirable traits. The vast majority of the time you tell yourself "I am different" or "I am better," you are hearing the ghost of false uniqueness.

One of the more frequently cited examples of false uniqueness in action is a study from 1981 done by Swedish psychologist Ola Svenson of American drivers. The most notable conclusion of the study was that 93% of participants claimed to be in the top half of all drivers in terms of skill.[34] A more recent AAA survey came to a similar conclusion: 73% of people think they are better than the average driver.[35]

Of course, it is mathematically impossible for 93% of all drivers to be in the top half in terms of skill, and it is *highly* unlikely for 73% of people to actually be better than average. We—all humans, not just the American variety—are just overly impressed with ourselves.

False uniqueness is one of the many behavioral quirks related to a general egocentric bias, which is recognized in behavioral science as one of humanity's foundational biases. We will more fully unpack the egocentric bias at the end of our journey in Growing, but for now it is enough

---

34   Ola Svenson, "Are We All Less Risky and More Skillful than Our Fellow Drivers," *Acta Psychologica* 47, no. 2 (February 1981): 143–48.

35   Ellen Edmonds, "More Americans Willing to Ride in Fully Self-Driving Cars," *AAA Newsroom*, January 24, 2018, https://newsroom.aaa.com/2018/01/americans-willing-ride-fully-self-driving-cars/.

to know that the egocentric bias is a tendency to rely too heavily on one's own perspective, which magnifies an individual's role in any given experience and leads to a higher opinion of oneself than reality would justify.[36]

Salespeople who allow the ghost of false uniqueness to do its work in convincing them that they are different use their perceived uniqueness as justification for all the reasons that the numbers game does not apply to them. After all, they are different, above average, special. Why wouldn't partners want to work with them? Why wouldn't prospects call them and fall over themselves for the opportunity to work with such a special person?

The punchline, unfortunately, is that you and I and everyone are not exceptional; we just *think* we are.

PROCRASTINATION

Procrastination is a short-term focus that leads to delay or postponement of action; if you hear yourself saying "I will do it later," you are hearing the ghost of procrastination.

My wife is a "dish-soaker." She will, with some frequency, leave her dishes in the sink so that they may soak before she cleans them, ostensibly because the soaking will make the cleaning easier. However, she soaks cereal bowls the same way she would a lasagna baking dish. In reality, soaking usually has nothing to do with cleaning and everything to do with the fact that she just does not want to clean the dish at the moment she puts it in the sink.

To be fair to my wife—and those readers who are dish-soakers themselves—we all do this. According to Dan Ariely, a

---

36   Brian Mullen, "Egocentric Bias in Estimates of Consensus," *Journal of Social Psychology* 121, no. 1 (1983): 31–38.

professor of psychology and behavioral economics at Duke University, procrastination causes problems for everyone.[37] In the short-term, we all prefer to delay the mundane, the challenging, or anything that is less fun so that we may do something novel, easy, or exciting instead. We do this with petty, insignificant things like dishes, and we do it with critically important things, like prospecting.

Behavioral science research connects human beings' tendency toward myopic procrastination to a present bias.[38] To be present-biased is to display a preference for immediate benefits over future benefits, going so far as to accept less value if it means more immediate satisfaction. To pervert a well-known saying, "a benefit in the present is worth two in the future." One outcome of this dynamic is the desire for instant gratification.

In evolutionary terms, our present bias likely developed due to the prehistoric uncertainty of the future. Today most of us can take for granted that the sun will rise tomorrow and that the foreseeable future is likely to be pretty similar to the present, but for most of our species' evolution—going back millions of years—tomorrow was very likely an unknown mystery that we struggled to conceptualize, let alone plan for.

Prospecting is anything but instantly gratifying. In relative terms, just about any other part of a salesperson's job can

---

37   Dan Ariely, "The Problem of Procrastination and Self-Control" in *Predictably Irrational: The Hidden Forces That Shape Our Decisions* (New York: HarperCollins, 2008).

38   A discussion paper in the March 2020 IZA Institute of Labor Economics Discussion Paper Series presents compelling evidence that procrastination is also driven by excessively optimistic beliefs about future demands on an individual's time. While this research adds justified nuance to the underpinnings of procrastination, our discussion will remain focused on the present bias as the primary driver of procrastination in the context of the sales cycle. Zachary Breig, Matthew Gibson, and Jeffrey G. Shrader, "Why Do We Procrastinate? Present Bias and Optimism," IZA Discussion Paper Series, no. 13060, March 2020.

provide more immediate satisfaction. Administrative work? Not really fun, but at least you have a definitive sense of accomplishment when you are done. Managing a current account? Interacting with a partner you already have an established relationship with can be an extremely rewarding experience. Doing research? You are learning, which is instantly gratifying, *and* you probably gain a sense of accomplishment. And so on.

Why do the thing that rarely pays off in the short term when you almost always have a choice to do something else that does? Whether the salesperson going about their job is consciously aware of such resistance or not, it can cause actual cold calling to be put off indefinitely, and measurable progress in sales along with it.

———

Deceived by the ghosts of fear of rejection, false uniqueness, and procrastination, salespeople fall into the trap of convincing themselves that the numbers game does not apply to them, that they can somehow find sustainable success without a process that guides an appropriate level of calling activity. However, this is demonstrably false, as the numerous studies and statistics cited throughout this chapter showcase.

Moreover, by taking responsibility for your innate human distaste for the possibility of being rejected, tasks that bruise the ego, and anything that is not instantly gratifying, you will also realize something powerful: in the end, prospecting success is completely within your control.

Let me be clear: the ghosts in the machine will not just go away because you are aware of them and take responsibility. But they can be dealt with.

Throughout this book, we will be discussing a variety of strategies to deal with the effects of the ghosts you will encounter along your journey through the sales cycle. More often than not, attempting to reason with them or tackle them head-on is not the best strategy. A head-on approach may help you intermittently push through their resistance, but is usually counterproductive, not to mention exhausting.

As for the deceitful ghosts, the most efficient way to respond is with some artful dodging.

In order to circumvent these ghosts, your best approach is a shift in mindset—a shift in how you look at the hard work of prospecting. While you cannot reason with or eliminate these ghosts, you can learn to reframe your understanding of the task at hand so that the deceitful ghosts are not as easily triggered. The key lies in what you choose to focus on.

The insight we discussed at the top of this chapter—that the primary driver of prospecting's low-probability nature is the chance of being in the right place at the right time— highlights one of the most underappreciated aspects of prospecting: you are *not* trying to convince every prospect to work with you.

Many salespeople approach every single prospecting call as a make-or-break moment, as a test of their selling ability. This attitude puts the burden of unrealistic expectations on the salesperson, setting them up for a failure when they inevitably underperform. Over time, the make-or-break approach erodes a salesperson's confidence in their abilities—which becomes a strong motivation to further pursue strategies to avoid prospecting and cold calling altogether.

No salesperson, no matter how skillful, should expect that an initial discussion with a prospect will result in expedited progress through the sales cycle. It is unrealistic for salespeople to expect more than a tiny fraction of prospects to be interested in what they are selling right out of the gate. A mentality focused on making a sale every time we speak with a prospect is what gives the deceitful ghosts their power, allowing them all the more opportunity to sap our enthusiasm for prospecting altogether.

To dodge the deceitful ghosts, let go of unrealistic expectations for your prospecting efforts. Stop expecting to make a sale or new best friend with each call you make; without such heights to fall from, the deceitful ghosts will create much less interference. Instead, strive to eliminate this make-or-break attitude and replace it with something that is grounded in prospecting's low-probability reality.

As salespeople, we can circumvent the influence of the deceitful ghosts by shifting our focus away from the success or failure of any one call or interaction—which is largely outside of our control—toward a focus on the process of building a pipeline full of prospects who have a high probability of wanting or needing what we are selling—which is completely inside our control.

Focusing on the process, after all, is what high-performing professionals do.

FOCUS ON THE PROCESS

> *"Life is a journey and not a destination."*
> —Lynn H. Hough

Athletic competition is one of humanity's oldest pastimes. Paleolithic cave paintings, such as the famous ones in

Lascaux, France, which are estimated to be more than fifteen thousand years old, contain captivating depictions of early human life. These walls illustrate how our ancestors imagined passage into the afterlife, how they hunted, and how they enjoyed their free time, including the occasional footrace and wrestling match.

Sports have come a long way since our ancestors first paid homage to competing for fun all those millennia ago. Fast-forward to the present, and sports have evolved into mature and finely tuned professional ecosystems that provide uniquely powerful laboratories for observing human behavior and performance, especially in regard to success.

If you were to survey the history of most professional sports, you would find players and teams in every league that consistently outperform their peers for extended periods of time. For contemporary American sports fans, the Golden State Warriors' recent run of dominance in the NBA, the New England Patriots' twenty-year run of NFL supremacy, and Michael Phelps' tear through the 2008–2016 Olympic Games will jump to mind.

The sustained dominance of certain players and teams leads one to wonder, "What do they know or do that everyone else does not?"

Putting aside the individual brilliance and unique talents of the most successful players and coaches (arguably, all professional sports leagues are full of equally brilliant and talented individuals), the secret to their sustained success is hiding in plain sight.

Watch a post-game interview with these most successful players and coaches, and, when asked about their performance, you are likely to hear things like "It's a long season,"

"We're taking it one game at a time," and "It's a process."
To the casual observer, these responses can feel canned
and halfhearted—and they often are—but that does not
make them any less insightful. Establishing and maintaining a focus on "the process" *is* the secret these high-performing professionals leverage to sustain success.

Throughout all levels of sports, the most successful players and teams focus on creating a foundation of habits
and routines—a process—that will promote continuous
improvement, and, ultimately, enable them to perform at
their best when the lights are brightest. Yes, it might be
a cliché, but for the most successful, the journey toward
success *is* the destination, much more so than the actual
realization of success.

**To focus on the process is to focus on getting better,
rather than focusing on the outcome of a single action or
performance.**

Focusing on outcomes creates an urgency to prove yourself over and over. Failure, therefore, is experienced as
an attack on your ego, emboldening the influence of the
deceitful ghosts. Conversely, focusing on the process
encourages learning and effort over instant success. In
turn, mistakes and failures along the way are embraced as
valuable feedback.

A process focus is an invaluable tool for the salesperson
during prospecting, helping clear the mind of the influence
of the deceitful ghosts that are such a problem:

- **Process focus blocks the ghost of fear of failure**
  - Focusing on the process will help mitigate any
    fear of rejection that creeps into your mind,
    steering attention away from the outcome

of a given call or meeting. In the big picture, building a thriving, sustainable business is the success that matters; all those "no" responses are not so bad when you keep this in mind.

- A process helps you keep the end in mind as a reason to call on enough prospects; if you maintain at least some semblance of organization along the way, you will succeed in spite of yourself.

- **Process focus removes the ghost of false uniqueness**

  - Focusing on the process removes impending threats to your ego and self-esteem. Instead of seeking validation in each individual circumstance and inevitably being let down, you are simply taking the steps outlined in the process without concern for any specific outcome other than doing what it takes to reach your end goal.

  - Behaving according to a set process also puts the focus back on the objective reality of the prospecting numbers game, helping immunize you to the promise of perceived superiority that can encourage you to slack off and believe your way will work despite evidence to the contrary.

- **Process focus takes control away from the ghost of procrastination**

  - Focusing on the process helps provide the motivation and determination needed to crank up the volume of your prospecting efforts.

  - A process will probably not help you find prospecting any more fun, but it will help you find a regular sense of accomplishment and gratification even when your efforts are not immediately rewarded. And that regular sense of accomplishment will help provide what you need to stick with your process beyond the short term.

If you are picking up what I am putting down—that salespeople can focus on the process to circumvent the effects of the deceitful ghosts—the next question that will come to mind is, "What is the best process for salespeople to adopt in the prospecting stage of the sales cycle?"

Good question.

In the prospecting stage, salespeople need a systematic and objective process to guide them as they play the numbers game. A process that provides feedback and actionable insight that will enable them to make adjustments and get better at finding the right prospects.

In other words, salespeople need to be *scientific* in their prospecting efforts.

It is often said that sales is more art than science. And while there is truth in stating that sales is an art, to say that its artistic nature is more important than the need to approach it with a sufficiently scientific process is little more than an excuse that allows the deceitful ghosts to roam unfettered through the machine.

Contrary to popular opinion, the application of scientific thought is not limited to what we traditionally think of as the sciences—biology, chemistry, physics, and so forth. Science—derived from the Latin word *scientia*, meaning *knowledge*—is a way to know things. It is no more than a systematic process that organizes a body of knowledge via testable explanations and predictions.

This systematic process—also known as *the scientific method*—may be used as a guiding light for anyone interested in better understanding any discipline. This, of course, includes the sales discipline.

THE SCIENTIFIC METHOD

The scientific method is the process for creating and executing an experiment using seven formally codified steps:

Observation *Make an observation.*

Question *Ask a question about the observation.*

Research *Research information about the observation.*

Hypothesis *Form a hypothesis, or testable prediction.*

Experiment *Design an experiment to test the hypothesis.*

Collection *Collect the results of the experiment.*

Iteration *Use the results to make new hypotheses or predictions, iterating until you are able to reliably predict the outcome.*

Note the cyclical nature of the scientific method: results lead to the revision or rejection of hypotheses or the creation of new ones, and the process begins again.

Importantly, the scientific method is designed to force a measure of objectivity by attempting to prove a hypothesis wrong, rather than seeking out information that will confirm its truth. This objectivity is precisely what salespeople need to circumvent the effects of the deceitful ghosts.

Humanity has leveraged the scientific method to great success and prosperity for more than 400 years. Why shouldn't salespeople take advantage of this tool as a process to help guide their prospecting efforts and find the methods that best keep themselves on track to generate sufficient call volume?

After all, what is prospecting but a type of experiment[39] aimed at finding the best way to identify those who want to do business with you?

Let's take a look at what leveraging the scientific method might look like for a cold-calling salesperson who isn't achieving their goal of thirty introductory meetings per quarter.

1. **Observation**
   - My current prospecting efforts are not translating into enough introductory meetings.
2. **Question**
   - How many prospects do I need to contact to meet my goal of 30 introductory meetings?
3. **Research**
   - Cold calling has an 8.21% response rate. (per Salesforce)

---

39   Although scientific studies generally control for irrelevant variables in ways that are not possible when prospecting, it is still informative and useful to think of optimizing your prospecting efforts in terms of these stages.

4. **Hypothesis**
   - If I make 365 calls,[40] I will meet my goal of 30 introductory meetings for the quarter. (365 x 8.21% = 30)

5. **Experiment**
   - Build a list and start calling.

6. **Collection of data**
   - Keep a running tally of total prospects contacted, noting each time you are successful in scheduling an introductory meeting.
   - After a period of time, review your results. How did your actual response rate compare with the 8.21% assumption you made based on research?

7. **Iteration**
   - Keep periodically reviewing your own personal response rate, making any necessary adjustments to your hypothesis until you can consistently predict whether you will achieve your meetings goal.

Granted, this example is oversimplified. (Using the scientific method does not have to be complicated!) Nonetheless, it illustrates the point: salespeople—just like scientists—can utilize the guiding principles of the scientific method to discover specifically how they are or are not reaching their goals, thereby turning their prospecting process into a fine-tuned instrument of success.

With purposeful, measured experimentation, maybe you

---

40   Again, we are oversimplifying here for sake of discussion. In order to realize the assumed 8.21% response rate, you may call 365 unique individuals, or you may use your 365 calls to focus on a smaller set of prospects which you will call multiple times within the quarter. Either way, the math holds and the point remains the same.

will discover that the solution for your issue is not call volume, but better targeting, or understanding which products and services are best to lead with. In any case, the scientific method is a proven process you can rely on to guide you toward achieving your goals with much more certainty.

It also affords you great flexibility in choosing a process that works for you. **Once you are aware of the influence of the deceitful ghosts and how a focus on outcomes can play right into the ego and the fears they feed on, all you need to do is create, test, and stick to your own process, which will help you move past their influence.**

Before we move on to the next section, here are a few additional blocking and tackling tips to help you on your way:

- Break down your prospecting volume into manageable blocks of time spread throughout the week; do NOT cram your prospecting efforts into full-day marathons, which will sap your energy, making it harder to connect with people and ignore the difficult emotions that can come with hearing "no" as often as is statistically likely.

- Set up prospecting time as you would any other appointment on your calendar and behave as though it is just as sacred as an actual meeting with a prospect or customer; it is. Without a sufficient amount of scheduled time for this crucial yet uncomfortable activity, it's easy to let it get pushed aside by other obligations.

- Although it does not really matter exactly when you implement your process, at the start of a new job or at the beginning of an annual sales cycle are natural opportunities to take time to consider your goals, decide how to measure your progress, and create a process for how to make them happen.

Outlining your scientific prospecting process need not be something that takes a lot of time or effort, either. Simply determine your goals for the upcoming month, quarter, year, etc., and spend a day—using the scientific method—to map out how you will test your effectiveness and ultimately get from here to where you want to be.

Speaking of goals, I have another insight to help you circumvent the deceitful ghosts. Not all goals are created equal. Some goals are smarter than others.

BE SMART

"Work smarter, not harder."
—Allen F. Morgenstern

One of the more daunting aspects of the prospecting stage of the sales cycle is its magnitude and lack of definition. To stare out at the expansive and undefined universe of prospects can feel like staring into the void.

Unlike the life cycles of other functions within a company—production, purchasing, finance, operations, and HR—or even the latter stages of the sales cycle, which are generally well defined and structured, prospecting is typically a chaotic mess.[41] Using the scientific method to bring order to the chaos is one half of the recipe for success in the prospecting stage. The other half is goal-setting.

---

41   *Of course* there are plenty of exceptions, especially in those industries that provide greater visibility into their composite companies. That said, chaos and lack of visibility is the general rule for most sales prospecting.

The scientific method is just a process; it will only get you to where you want to go if you have an effective goal to work with.

Set effective goals and the scientific method will work wonders for you. Feed it ineffective or bad goals, and you will just be spinning your wheels, if not worse off than when you began. As effectiveness expert Stephen Covey says, "If the ladder is not leaning against the right wall, every step we take just gets us to the wrong place faster."

So how does one go about setting effective goals? Thankfully, that part's easy. Just be SMART.

SMART GOALS

While there are various goal-setting methodologies, SMART goals rise above the rest in their ability to facilitate the development and implementation of an action plan. In order to be SMART, goals need to meet the following criteria. For consistency with our scientific method example above, we will use thirty introductory meetings per quarter as an example goal.

- *Specific—What is the specific goal?*
  - *30 introductory meetings for the quarter*
- *Measurable—Is the goal quantifiable?*
  - *Yes, 30 is a benchmark I can measure against.*
- *Achievable—Is the goal achievable given the available resources?*
  - *Yes; I have a phone, and if I contact 365 prospects, which is between 5 and 6 per day,[42] I should be able to achieve this goal.*

---

42 Assuming a thirteen-week quarter and five business days per week

- *Relevant*—Is the goal in line with other variables and factors, given the circumstances?
  - In our simplified example, yes, because we are only concerned with meeting our goal of 30 introductory meetings. If our circumstances dictated that we spend the majority of our time expanding our share of wallet by selling additional products and services to a defined set of current customers, 365 prospect calls in a quarter might not be in line with those circumstances.
- *Time-bound*—Does the goal have a target date?
  - Yes, I will know whether I have succeeded or failed by the end of the quarter.

These five criteria dovetail nicely with the scientific method's objectivity, creating a synergy that will increase the effectiveness of your efforts in the prospecting stage, as well as all subsequent stages of the sales cycle.

The scientific method may provide the focus on the process you need to circumvent the deceitful ghosts and get out of your own way, but you need to be SMART in setting your goals if you want to maximize its effectiveness. If you want to bring order to the prospecting chaos and make sure the ladder you are climbing as the sales cycle unfolds takes you where you want to go, setting SMART goals is the very first step you need to take.

BONUS: MERE EXPOSURE EFFECT

If you have ever walked down an aisle of the grocery store, noticed a product on the shelf, and effortlessly recited its jingle as you add it to your shopping cart, you are familiar with *the mere exposure effect*.

The mere exposure effect is a psychological phenomenon by which people tend to develop a preference for things merely because they are familiar with them. Advertisers have been using it for decades as a foundational way to keep their brands and products top-of-mind—and therefore preferred by consumers.

The mere exposure effect is yet another reason why you need to be consistent and persistent with your prospecting efforts. By simply making yourself familiar to a prospect through repetitive "exposure" over time, you will begin to create a new default in their mind, one that perceives you as a known entity—one that they are less antagonistic toward and find easier to like. And being liked, as we are about to discover in the next phase of the sales cycle, is critical if you hope to have success in sales.

———

We have spent considerable time and effort in this chapter to make a pretty simple point: prospecting is a numbers game, and a low-probability one at that. If you want to be successful in prospecting—and subsequently, successful in your sales career—you will have to contact a lot of prospects. There are other important aspects of prospecting—networking, targeting, timing of calls, etc.—but none as critical as sheer volume.

Evolution has predisposed human beings toward fear of rejection, a false sense of uniqueness, and procrastination. These deceitful ghosts sap the average person's energy for prospecting and disincentivize them to actually make those crucial calls.

By setting SMART goals and using the principles of the scientific method to focus on developing and following a process for contacting as many prospects as possible, you will be able to circumvent the effects of these deceitful ghosts and increase the effectiveness of your prospecting efforts. A process focus will also relieve you of the high pressure to perform that comes with an outcome focus, setting the table for you to find your long-term prospecting groove, even when you experience day-to-day setbacks.

Once you have set up and begun to execute in the prospecting phase according to your process, it is only a matter of time before you get your foot in the door and move to the next stage of the sales journey, Relationship Building—where we will discover that the way most salespeople go about building professional relationships is all wrong.

RELATIONSHIP BUILDING

Imagine you are at a party.

Maybe it is a big party with tons of people, multiple bars, and a DJ playing the kind of music that gets you in the mood to enjoy yourself. Maybe it is a simple backyard get-together with a well-stocked ice chest and your favorite kind of meat on the grill. Or maybe it is something else altogether—wherever you can imagine that you are in your element.

Take a moment to visualize the atmosphere around you. Is it daytime or nighttime? Where are you: in the club, at someone's house? Who else is there? If you are drinking, what are you drinking? Really paint the picture in your mind.

Now, imagine that you have been engrossed in a particularly interesting conversation with a good friend. At this moment, your friend has just excused themselves to grab another drink, and you find yourself alone with your

GHOSTS IN THE MACHINE

thoughts. You are enjoying yourself. This party fits you like an old glove. It is comfortable. It is easy for you to be at.

As you are enjoying your moment of Zen,[43] someone approaches you from across the way. You are not familiar with this person, but they come straight over to you and confidently introduce themselves. Unsure where this is going, you politely respond and ask them what's up. And, out of nowhere, this stranger—smack in the middle of this awesome party—unpacks an easel and a presentation titled, "The Merits of Friendship with Me."

Taken aback by what is happening, you are only able to grab brief snippets of the presentation: "...93% punctuality rate...season ticket holder to blah blah...rated five stars in friendship satisfaction per yadda yadda..." Before you can get your bearings, this person has already raced through half of their presentation.

How do you feel now?

Are you still enjoying yourself? Are you still comfortable? Is this party still easy to be at?

Before you dismiss the admittedly ridiculous premise of this visualization exercise, let me ask you a question: how is this scenario fundamentally different than the typical interaction that many salespeople have with prospects when they first meet?

RELATIONSHIPS ARE NOT BUILT RATIONALLY

"It has been said that man is a rational animal.
All my life I have been searching for evidence
which could support this."
—Bertrand Russell

---

43   *tipping hat in acknowledgement to the Daily Show*

Decision-makers care about many factors when making a purchasing decision. They care about features, advantages, and benefits. They care about speed and certainty of execution. They care about price. They care about brand reputation. They care about all these things—and it is true, all of these things are important—but these things are not the primary drivers in their decision-making calculus.

More often than not, the most important factor in making a purchasing decision is the connection an individual decision-maker has with a salesperson.

Consumer decision-making is 30% rational and **70%** emotional.[45]

According to a 2015 Corporate Executive Board analysis of 4,960 business-to-business customers, **53%** of customer loyalty is driven by the individual salesperson.[44]

44   Per Corporate Executive Board Challenger Workshop Presentation (2015).
45   Gallup, *2017 Global Emotions Report*, 2017, https://news.gallup.com/reports/212678/2017-global-emotions-report.aspx.

Salespeople may find short-term success by leading with features, advantages, and benefits—especially if they are fortunate enough to represent a truly differentiated or unique product or service—but long-term success is built on the relationship between buyer and seller. More than any other factor, this personal connection is what drives the sustainability and longevity of professional relationships.

Approaching prospects with easel and presentation in hand, all geared up to debate on the rational merits of their product or service, is one of the most fundamental mistakes salespeople make in trying to establish and nurture professional relationships.

Despite their paramount importance, most sales systems either take the fundamentals of relationship building for granted or neglect them altogether. Instead, these systems focus on other aspects of the sales cycle, like uncovering needs, competitive positioning, value creation, pipeline management, and so on. Basically everything appears on the sales guidance menu *except* the nuances of relationship building.

This is a shame, because when it comes to interacting with other human beings, we weight relationships and emotions more heavily than rational argument. We must remember that prospects and customers are emotional creatures first and rational decision-makers second. In many ways, the whole sales cycle is primarily built upon emotional, not logical, relationships.

I am dedicating this chapter to understanding a more effective way to establish and build professional relationships precisely because of salespeople's tendency to focus on rational arguments and precisely because sales guides generally skip over the relationship-building stage of the sales cycle altogether.

Though clichés about first impressions can feel tired, when it comes to relationship building within the sales cycle, they are still very applicable. The initial impressions that prospects form about you—which they will do within moments of meeting you—have a long-lasting effect on the trajectory of your relationship with them and just how willing they are to consider working with you.

Initiating a sales call with rational arguments in favor of the product or service you are selling—with little or no consideration for relationship building—is the best way to spoil your first impression. Doing so is akin to building a house without a foundation. Just like that tilting, unstable house, professional relationships that lack a strong interpersonal connection are liable to fall apart when they hit the slightest friction.

As is the case with decision-making in general, approximately 70% of the initial impression you make on your prospects will be emotional, far outweighing the rational considerations many salespeople spend their time and energy focusing on.

Unfair as it might be, these first impressions are the deciding factor in whether or not you are even provided the opportunity to build a relationship. Furthermore, if a professional relationship is established without a strong interpersonal connection, at the first sign of friction, both parties will be incentivized to hold something back, unable to fully trust the other, leading to suboptimal outcomes, if not a parting of ways. And, as you are probably aware, friction between buyers and sellers is *unavoidable*.

With this in mind, how, in those crucial first moments, can we go about establishing a strong connection with our prospects?

The answer is simple. Before you do anything else, you must make a friend.

MAKING FRIENDS

> *"The way to go from discord to harmony is to go from concentrating on differences to concentrating on similarities."*
> *—Tony Robbins*

Very broadly speaking, social friendships typically develop naturally, without any kind of concentrated effort or practice; you simply click with someone or you do not. In the world of professional relationship building, we usually do not have that luxury, and will need to be a bit more deliberate in our approach. Yet if we put that rather large difference to the side, making a professional contact or friendship is not fundamentally different from making a social friend. And thanks to behavioral science, we know how.

In his groundbreaking book *Influence*, Robert Cialdini introduces six persuasion principles that impact decision-making. While each of these principles are valuable in their own right, in our discussion of making friends, one in particular provides a guiding light: *liking*.

It may sound obvious, but for those of us who want proof, Cialdini's research demonstrates that human beings are far more willing to consent to a request—such as a meeting request—from someone they like. An example from Cialdini's Influence at Work website illustrates the point.

In a series of negotiation studies carried out between MBA students at two well-known business schools, some groups were told, "Time is money. Get straight down to business." In this group, around 55% were able to come to an agreement.

A second group, however, was told, "Before you begin negotiating, exchange some personal information with each other. Identify a similarity you share in common then begin negotiating." In this group, 90% of the participants were able to come to successful and agreeable outcomes that were typically worth 18% more to both parties.[46]

As the cliché goes, people work with people they like.

According to Cialdini, people that we like benefit from or take advantage of some combination of five liking factors that tend to draw us to them: *attractiveness*; *similarity*; *compliments*; *contact and cooperation*; and *conditioning and association*. Although all five are important in being liked, I would argue that similarity is the factor that is most applicable for salespeople in the early stages of relationship building, and that is what we will focus on here.

The liking factor of similarity basically means that we humans tend to like those people that have similar interests, opinions, tastes, personalities, etc. to our own. If you take a moment to think about the people you consider your friends, it is a good bet that those people are pretty similar to you. While different people of course weight different types of similarity as more or less important, you will probably be able to find some overarching similarities amongst every friend group.

---

46   "The Science of Persuasion: Six Principles of Persuasion," Influence at Work, https://www.influenceatwork.com/6-principles-of-persuasion/

If you want to become professional friends with your prospects and customers, you will do well to find similarities with them, too.

Salespeople who seek opportunities to highlight similarities when approaching their prospects frequently find themselves more well-received, more liked. In turn, they find more open doors and more opportunities to win business, which is the ultimate goal.

Of course, it is not enough *just* to be liked. As a professional rather than a social friend, over time you must demonstrate that you are able to provide value—eventually you must deliver, or at least explain how you will deliver with those rational arguments we discussed earlier. **However, being liked is a prerequisite to these factors. Being liked is the spark that lights the relationship flame.**

Only after you are liked by your prospects are they likely to give your rational case for your products and services a fair trial.

Unfortunately, salespeople too often lead their relationship-building efforts with all the rational reasons a given prospect or customer should work with them, anticipating initial meetings as they would a debate competition. Although the belief that leading with rational arguments is the best way to grab a prospect's attention persists, this represents a fundamental misunderstanding of how relationships are built and how decisions are made.

Imagine if you did this in your social life. Imagine if, like in our thought exercise from the beginning of this chapter, you were the one whipping an easel out every time you met someone new, permanent marker in hand, prepared to prove to them why you would be such a good friend. You probably would not have very many friends—and those who did stick around would likely be of the transactional and shallow variety.

You cannot afford for your prospects to see you as that kind of professional friend. **So, do not make the mistake of treating your first meeting with a prospect as a purely rational interaction.**

The human connection you make with them is paramount— and unfortunately, making that connection can be made all the more difficult by how our minds work. This is because, no matter how nice of a person you are, or how well-liked you are in your already-established relationships, prospects will initially view you as an antagonist.

As salespeople, our job is to persuade people to make some kind of change to what they are currently doing. Our job is to compete against their current vendor, to convince them the status quo is not good enough—which is exactly what it means to antagonize. If we jump out of the gate debate-team style, we are only heightening that impression.

Based on research originally done by Lee Ross and Constance Stillinger,[47] when a proposal, idea, or opinion originates from an antagonist, it is immediately devalued. This is known in behavioral science as *reactive devaluation*. Like it or not, your prospects will instinctually discount all the valuable things you share about your product or service until they no longer see you as an antagonist.

---

47   In 1988 Ross and Stillinger asked pedestrians in the US whether they would support a drastic bilateral nuclear arms reduction program. If they were told the proposal came from President Ronald Reagan, 90% said it would be favorable or even-handed to the United States; if they were told the proposal came from a group of unspecified policy analysts, 80% thought it would be favorable or even; but, if respondents were told it came from Mikhail Gorbachev, only 44% thought it would be favorable or neutral to the United States. See Lee Ross and Constance Stillinger, "Barriers to Conflict Resolution," *Negotiation Journal* 7, no. 4 (October 1991): 389–404.

When salespeople launch into their product or service's features, advantages, and benefits too soon, unfortunately, they are automatically reinforcing the idea that they are an antagonist rather than a friend. This is the exact opposite of giving the prospect time to become comfortable and familiar with them, and it is likely to reinforce resistance that further handicaps the rational approach to relationship building.

I will say it again: only after you have established a relationship with your customer or prospect—after they overcome their initial resistance enough to like you—will all the incredible value you have to offer be properly appreciated.

So, if we are to be liked by and make friends with our prospects, how will we push past their instinctually antagonistic view of us?

The truth is that "it's complicated," and there are a lot of variables to consider. The most important of those variables will be covered a little later in this chapter. But first, we must understand how humans actually think.

The human mind is not as rational as it is lazy.

LAZINESS IS NOT A BUG, IT IS *THE* FEATURE

> *"Effort comes at a cost."*
> —Daniel Kahneman

Thinking is hard.

The human mind is not a fully optimized computer thinking through each and every circumstance in a reasoned and logical fashion. In practical terms, the brain functions much more like an association machine. What our minds really do, the vast majority of the time, is remain on a kind of autopilot, leading us to simply do and think what we usually do and think. Our thoughts and beliefs are guided toward the path of least resistance and biased toward the information that is most easily accessed.

These ideas about how our thoughts work have been distilled by the behavioral science community into three concepts—*the law of least effort, the availability bias*, and *System 1/System 2 thinking*. Understanding them is key to relationship-building success, and yet they are radically underappreciated in the sales world. In order to get better at connecting with our prospects and customers, we will take a closer look at each concept in turn, as well as how the three come together to form a holy trinity of relationship-building prowess.

THE PATH OF LEAST RESISTANCE

Human beings are lazy.

Given almost any set of circumstances, we will seek out ways to exert as little effort as possible as we make our way through life. And although society generally frowns upon laziness—going so far as to cast it a deadly sin—when seen through the lens of behavioral science, being lazy is much more about economy of effort than it is some kind of degenerate slothfulness.

In fact, laziness is baked into the very fabric of the universe.

Newton's first law of motion states: "An object at rest stays at rest, and an object in motion stays in motion, with the same speed and in the same direction, unless acted upon by an unbalanced force." This natural law describes laziness through the scientific lens of least resistance.

Being objects in the universe, we, too, are driven to follow the path of least resistance. This is our first key relationship-building concept, and it provides lots of context for the fairly obvious conclusion that we will avoid hard work whenever possible.

LAW OF LEAST EFFORT

In his 2011 tour de force, Thinking, Fast and Slow, *behavioral science founding father Daniel Kahneman—whom we met in our discussion of cognitive biases in the introduction—writes of "A general 'law of least effort' [that] applies to cognitive as well as physical exertion. The law asserts that if there are several ways of achieving the same goal, people will eventually gravitate to the least demanding course of action. In the economy of action, effort is a cost, and the acquisition of skill is driven by the balance of benefits and costs. Laziness is built deep into our nature."[48]*

We are lazy because effort comes at a cost. That cost is the energy required to concentrate and focus our attention, and that energy is a limited resource. When given a choice among options, we instinctively choose the least demanding so that our energy is conserved; we may need it in the future. Human beings do this because it has proven to be an evolutionarily successful strategy.

The better we come to understand ourselves and the universe we live in, the clearer it becomes that the law of least effort is everywhere, though sometimes it is known by different names:

---

48   Daniel Kahneman, *Thinking, Fast and Slow* (New York: Farrar, Straus and Giroux, 2011), 35.

- *The principle of least action dictates the flow of water and electricity*
- *The principle of least effort governs information-seeking*
- *Psychology has the law of least work*
- *The study of linguistics calls it Zipf's law*
- *And so on...*

The law of least effort is vital to the study of behavioral science. It is so powerful that it is deterministic of human behavior, which is to say, it is predictive of what people will do. Given a choice between similarly rewarding options, people learn to avoid those that require more work or effort.[49]

It turns out that often, the path of least resistance is simply the most efficient way to go. **Taking the lazy way is not a bug in our behavioral code—it is a core feature.** And, most pertinent from a sales perspective, our laziness extends beyond the physical realm. People are cognitively lazy as well.

This leads nicely to our second key point in this section: thinking, like physical activity, takes effort.

ACCESSIBILITY

A recent psychology study proposes that the average human has around 6,200 thoughts per day.[50] Frankly, that is way too many thoughts. People simply do not have the time or energy to thoroughly assess that many thoughts

---

49   C. L. Hull, *Principles of Behavior: An Introduction to Behavior Theory* (New York: Appleton-Century-Crofts, 1943).

50   Julie Tseng and Jorden Poppenk, "Brain meta-state transitions demarcate thoughts across task contexts exposing the mental noise of trait neuroticism," *Nature Communications* 11, no. 3480 (2020).

each and every day. If a person tried to spend the time and energy to rationally dissect every thought that crossed their mind and critique every belief they held about the world, they would be totally overwhelmed.

Given this massive volume of thoughts, our minds have developed information-gathering shortcuts that allow us to get through the day, saving our mental energy for only the most mission-critical decision-making. These shortcuts are known to behavioral science as heuristics: efficient approaches that are generally successful at reaching immediate goals but are not necessarily optimal or rational.

Heuristics work quickly and preserve energy, but they carry an inherent risk of error. One of the primary errors these mental shortcuts create are cognitive biases, which we defined in the introduction as patterns of deviation from rational judgement.

Our minds leverage heuristics to help us more efficiently (read: more lazily) use our limited mental energy. And one of our most efficient heuristics is the use of mental associations, which form the foundation of our second key relationship-building concept: *availability bias.*

AVAILABILITY BIAS

Viewed through the lens of behavioral science, the availability bias is a heuristic (or mental shortcut, if you prefer) that relies on easily accessed information that comes to mind when evaluating a given situation—such as the immediate accessibility of a first impression.

Tversky and Kahneman describe availability as "estimate[ing] frequency or probability by the ease with which instances or associations could be brought to mind." In simpler terms, the human mind guesses the likelihood that an event will happen by using easily recalled memories as a reference.

Furthermore, the availability of a thought becomes a proxy for its importance. We tend to assume that easily accessed thoughts jump to mind because they are important, whether or not this is actually the case.

Cialdini has this to say about how our minds process information: "The brain's operations arise fundamentally and inescapably from raw associations. Just as amino acids can be called the building blocks of life, associations can be called the building blocks of thought."[51]

Most of the time, people do not think about the best or most rational course of action; the first thing they think about is the idea or course of action that is already associated in their mind with the topic at hand.

The stickiness of first impressions highlights the power of mental associations—like the availability bias—and why they matter to our efforts to get prospects to like us. As is clear to anyone who has made a bad first impression, associations based on initial impressions are not always correct or even useful. And yet, they persist.

It has become common knowledge that "people tend to form split-second impressions with regard to others' presumably stable characteristics, such as trustworthiness and competence."[52] These first impressions are based on superficial traits like appearances and simple behaviors (e.g., a handshake), and they have a disproportionate effect on the opinions we form of others.

---

51   Robert Cialdini, *Pre-Suasion: A Revolutionary Way to Influence and Persuade* (New York: Simon & Schuster, 2016), 99.
52   Irmak Olcaysoy Okten, "Studying First Impressions: What to Consider?," Association for Psychological Science, *Observer*, January 31, 2018, https://www.psychologicalscience.org/observer/studying-first-impressions-what-to-consider.

Critically, these knee-jerk reactions tend to be tricky to reverse. Research shows that, although people may rationally update a first impression based on later impressions that run counter to the first, they are still shown to have instinctual reactions that align with their initial impression.[53] Thus, associations based on initial impressions can persist and affect interpersonal interactions in significant ways, even when perceivers themselves are convinced that they have changed their impressions in light of new information.[54]

The mental heuristic of relying on associations might be evolutionarily efficient for you and your prospects, but these associations can absolutely make your sales job harder. **If a prospect does not like you at a first meeting, every proposal and fact you bring up will be associated via the availability bias with that original negative impression in their mind, as that impression is still the most readily accessed.**

You can already see how big of a problem this can be. And we will discuss how to avoid this stumbling block in more depth soon—but first, let's get to our final key relationship-building concept.

RUNNING ON AUTOPILOT

Daniel Kahneman coined the phrase "fast and frugal" to describe the way our minds work when it comes to making decisions—yet another way of saying "efficient" or "lazy."[55]

53   Olcaysoy Okten, "Studying First Impressions."
54   Aiden P. Gregg, Beate Seibt, and Mahzarin R. Banaji, "Easier Done Than Undone: Asymmetry in the Malleability of Implicit Preferences," *Journal of Personality and Social Psychology* 90, no. 1 (2006): 1-20; and Thomas C. Mann and Melissa J. Ferguson, "Can We Undo Our First Impressions?: The Role of Reinterpretation in Reversing Implicit Evaluations," *Journal of Personality and Social Psychology* 108, no. 6 (2015): 823-49.
55   Kahneman, *Thinking, Fast and Slow.*

Like Cialdini, Kahneman also recognizes the importance of associations and availability as foundational to human thought, and he goes a bit further in fleshing out the idea.

According to Kahneman, our minds—our association machines—have evolved two separate systems for processing the stimulation we receive from the environment. *System 1* is our autopilot function, streamlining day-to-day decision-making by leveraging what is readily available in our minds, such as pre-linked associations. *System 2*, our rational-thought mode, is only engaged when thinking becomes harder. We typically use System 2 when a pre-linked association isn't readily available and we actually have to stop and think about a decision.

The System 1/System 2 dynamic is our third key relationship building concept.

SYSTEM 1 AND SYSTEM 2

Based on the law of least effort and guided by the availability bias, we are geared toward thought patterns that make it easier for our association machines to run smoothly. Therefore, we have a preference for those ideas that confirm rather than conflict with our pre-linked associations. This is known as confirmation bias; we will discuss it more in Changing, but for now, know that it is one of the main mechanisms System 1 uses in being "fast and frugal" in processing information.

System 1 operates automatically and quickly, with little or no effort.

- *System 1 thinking is instinctive and emotional.*
- *System 1 takes shortcuts, such as associations and other heuristics.*

- *System 1 only considers the here and now and has no sense of voluntary control.*
- *System 1 is prone to biases and systematic errors.*
- *System 1 is where the ghosts in the machine reside.*

System 2 allocates attention to effortful mental activities, including complex computations.

- *System 2 thinking is deliberative and logical.*
- *System 2 involves conscious reasoning about beliefs, choices, and decisions.*
- *System 2 considers the future and is in charge of self-control.*
- *System 2 has the ability to counter System 1 biases—if it is engaged.*

When things are going smoothly, System 1 runs the show and System 2 rests in standby mode. When System 1 runs into trouble, System 2 is mobilized, shifting our thought process into a more analytical mode. It is important to keep in mind that we are not always aware of shifts back and forth between System 1 and System 2 thinking.

Instinctual feelings turn into beliefs and impulses, which turn into voluntary actions, when unconfirmed ideas and impressions from System 1 are endorsed by System 2. Right or wrong, most of the time System 2 usually acts as an apologist for System 1, rather than a critic—only reinforcing the stickiness of associations like first impressions.

Sticking with our *human beings are lazy* theme, behavioral science essentially tells us that most of the time, we would rather stay on autopilot, leveraging our System 1 thinking, because doing so is *way* easier than having to stop and think about something.

———

The law of least effort, availability bias, and System 1/ System 2 are three of behavioral science's foundational concepts. The lazy interplay between these three—seeking the path of least resistance, which drives our mental association machine and creates bias toward what is readily available, which we then treat preferentially and end up valuing more despite its irrational roots—is responsible for many of the feelings and perceptions we have, including the people to whom we take a liking.

These key brain patterns typically manifest themselves to haunt relationship building in the form of *representativeness*—a term that encompasses both of our lazy ghosts.

IF-THEN

"By their very nature, heuristic shortcuts will produce biases..."
—Daniel Kahneman

Representativeness is a mental shortcut (heuristic) originally discussed by Kahneman and Amos Tversky.[56] Put simply, our brains' representativeness behavior assesses the similarity of objects—or people, in the sales context we are concerned with—to a master prototype that, in the lazy mind, *represents* each individual within that group.

---

56   These two are kind of a big deal in behavioral science—if that hasn't already become obvious.

For example, if you are in the checkout line at the grocery store and you are standing behind someone wearing hospital scrubs, you will most likely assume they work in a hospital. Although that assumption is pretty likely to be true, in reality, you do not *know* whether they work in a hospital, whether they are on their way to a costume party, or whether they just find hospital scrubs comfortable to wear when running errands. Nevertheless, your brain is going to group the person in front of you into the category of hospital workers, because that is what their outfit *represents*.

Representativeness is particularly important in the context of the sales cycle, relationship building, and our efforts to be liked by our prospects and customers because it often colors our first impressions.

At the risk of oversimplifying, representativeness works like a mental "if-then" function. System 1 looks out at the world, scanning for and processing a variety of sensory information. In doing so, it runs the sensory information gathered through a relatively simple filter: "If" something looks/feels/smells/tastes/sounds like X, "then" it probably *is* X.

In relation to our liking discussion above, if someone looks *similar* to you, then most likely, you will subconsciously be more inclined to like them. Of course there are many nuances to what the brain might consider "similar" and how conscious thought affects these underlying impressions, but that is the basic gist.

Representativeness is a remarkably effective mental shortcut, but it—like all shortcuts—is prone to errors. **Although it helps us navigate through the world and is relatively inexpensive from a cognitive load standpoint, this brain** behavior pattern also gives birth to the lazy ghosts in the machine: *stereotyping* and *in-group bias.*

These ghosts motivate prospects to make decisions based on superficial impressions while deemphasizing more rational considerations. And they are major sources of the resistance that salespeople feel when trying to develop professional friendships with their prospects. Salespeople must learn to understand and connect with these ghosts if they hope to build successful relationships with their prospects.

STEREOTYPING

Stereotyping is a plague on modern society.

In too many instances—racism, sexism, classism, etc.—stereotypes have earned their despicable reputation as facilitators of horrendous acts of prejudice, oppression, and violence. However, based on the latest empirical evidence, behavioral scientists theorize that the mental act of stereotyping is so deeply and problematically ingrained in our System 1 thinking because it was once a successful evolutionary strategy.

To stereotype a group of people is to hold an overgeneralized belief about them. Typically, a stereotype is assigned to a person based on those knee-jerk initial impressions we discussed earlier. Hence the colloquialism "judging the book by its cover," which is exactly what this lazy ghost is all about.

Over the course of hundreds of thousands of years, humankind learned to triangulate limited pieces of sensory information when making critical, often split-second, life-and-death decisions. For example, when our ancient ancestors were foraging for food, they learned to recognize what poisonous plants looked, smelled, and tasted like. When they came across a new, unrecognized thing that looked, smelled, or tasted like those known poisonous things, our ancestors simply avoided it as though it were the poisonous thing and lived to see another day.

Of course, this strategy carries a risk of false positive. But in the times in which our ancestors evolved, it was far better to miss out on something edible than it was to risk death. The same went for our interactions with other human beings. Our ancestors needed to be able to determine if a stranger in the distance was a friend or foe by making split-second assumptions based on what they looked, sounded, and smelled like.

Sadly, despite the fact that our world is infinitely more nuanced now, our brains can still be swayed by the involuntary instinct to judge someone in a split second. Stereotyping still guides our initial impressions of the people we meet—and theirs of us. Know that your prospects will instinctively stereotype you based on their initial impressions, whether right or wrong.

There is a wide variety of volumes dedicated to classifying the origins of our stereotyping instincts, tracing their negative impacts, and providing alternatives to these behaviors—volumes that are worth your time and attention, whether you find yourself the target of negative stereotyping or are looking to learn how to understand and mitigate the effects it has on others. Unfortunately, here, we do not have the space and time to properly account for the full breadth of stereotyping's impact on human relations.

In this chapter, we are focusing on a narrow band of stereotyping that has a specific and disproportionate impact on your sales efforts: those lazy, uninformed first impressions that you have the ability to influence.

Though there will be prospects and customers who have ignorant preconceptions of you based on things about you that you cannot and should not change, many of the elements involved in the first impression you make on others *are* within your control. As psychologist Leil Lowndes so eloquently states in her book, *How to Talk to Anyone: 92 Little Tricks for Big Success in Relationships*, "Every smile, every frown, every syllable you utter, every arbitrary choice of word that passes between your lips, can draw others toward you, or make them want to run away."[57]

Here is a quick example. You may emphasize your trustworthiness when initially meeting prospects by making eye contact with them 60–70% of the time during a meeting with them.[58] Make too little eye contact and you will give the impression that you are nervous or untrustworthy; make too much eye contact and you will make the other person uncomfortable.

Most people have never put much thought into how much eye contact to make with others—even if they understand that it is important to "look people in the eye"—yet it has a profound impact on how other people respond to our behavior. Eye contact is one of those elements of a first impression that is fully within your control; use it wisely.

Along with superficial traits like your appearance, other simple behaviors like eye contact—the way you shake hands, whether you smile or frown, whether you are sitting

57   Leil Lowndes, *How to Talk to Anyone: 92 Little Tricks for Big Success in Relationships* (Chicago: Contemporary Books, 2003).
58   Noah Zandan, "Eye Contact—A Declining Communications Tool?," *Quantified Communications Blog*, Quantified, https://www.quantified.ai/blog/eye-contact-a-declining-communications-tool/.

upright or slouching—count among the 70% of decision-making elements that are emotional. And, unlike physical traits, simple behavioral cues are completely within your control. **The initial impressions you make based on these elements will have a disproportionate effect on the opinions of others—on the stereotypes they associate with you—dictating whether or not your prospects will view you as similar to them and whether or not they will find you worthy of liking.**

One way or another, your prospects will have an impression of you that is largely driven by knee-jerk reactions. The question is: now that you are aware of the impact of those first few moments, what first impressions will you provide for them?

IN-GROUP BIAS

In his best-selling follow-up to *Influence*, *Pre-suasion,* Cialdini expands on the similarity aspect of liking by introducing a concept he calls *the unity principle.* According to the unity principle, individuals use categories—race, ethnicity, nationality, family, political and religious affiliation, etc.—to define themselves and their groups. According to Cialdini, "A key characteristic of these categories is that their members tend to feel at one with, merged with, the others."[59]

This is the essence of our second lazy ghost—in-group bias—and it hearkens back to our Social Leap discussion in the introduction. As humanity's social evolution toward cooperation and the need to belong blossomed, humans also grew to form distinctions between those in "their" group and those in "other" groups.

People and groups instinctively prefer and more quickly

---

59   Robert Cialdini, *Pre-Suasion*, 175.

accept those who look and sound like they do, deeming those included the "in-group," worthy of special treatment. The in-group bias ghost simultaneously drives preferential treatment of those in the "in-group" and prejudicial treatment of those in the "out-group." As far as the in-group bias ghost sees the world, it really *is* "us versus them."

While the in-group bias is not inherently good or bad—it is no more than a cognitive shortcut that was once evolutionarily effective—the "us versus them" mentality it promotes has, along with stereotyping, had nasty and tragic consequences throughout history, consequences that persist as strongly as ever to this very day.

Before we go any further, let me be clear: certain categories—the country in which you were born, the color of your skin, or the religious affiliation you were born into jump to mind, but there are plenty of others—are absolutely unacceptable for people to judge others on, although we must acknowledge that this still happens all too frequently. In truth, differences like these deserve to be celebrated as part of the infinite variety of humankind, the variety that brings richness to all of our lives.

Out-group prejudices are an unfair reality that too many people confront all too frequently, and sales is no exception. That said, a full treatment of humanity's instincts to sort people into in-groups and out-groups is beyond the scope of our present discussion. For more in-depth learning about the behavioral influence of out-group prejudices on human relations, I again suggest you look to the many experts writing about these issues, from the behavioral science community and the wider world. People of all walks of life create content about prejudices they have experienced and what can be done to combat them, and the best thing to do to learn more is to start listening to them.

Further, in our discussion of the impact the in-group bias has on relationship building, in no way am I suggesting that salespeople pander to those who treat them as inferior, or try to hide parts of themselves in order to fit into a prospect or customer's small-minded view of the world. Sadly, there will be some cases where someone's out-group prejudices ruin a professional friendship before it begins. In those cases, the responsibility for that failure of basic human decency falls on the other person, not you.

In this book, given our focus on applying behavioral science to enhance the impact of our efforts throughout the sales cycle, we are going to focus on leveraging the human mind's in-group bias by figuring out which categories and in-groups we may be able to find *in common* with our customers. And while sometimes this can be a lost cause through no fault of the salesperson, in many cases, opportunities abound.

There are plenty of ways that people group themselves that have to do with behavior and choice rather than identity. Things as mundane as personal interests, whether or not you are married, whether or not you have children, where you currently live, shop and play, where you went to school and what you studied, and so on are in-groups that you may have in common with a prospect. If you focus on building a connection and finding similarity—rather than pushing your rational arguments—you will often discover that you already have at least one in-group in common with your prospects and customers.

Being recognized as part of an in-group is one of the strongest mitigants to a prospect's initial impression of you as an antagonist, and one of the best ways to demonstrate your similarity to and unity with them. I am consistently impressed, after beating my head against a wall for some time trying to get the attention of a prospect, at how freely and openly I am welcomed after connecting the dots that we went to the same school.

Leveraging this lazy ghost in your favor is actually quite straightforward. **The more you are perceived as a member of any of various categories that your prospects identify as, the more open and receptive they will be to you.**

This is precisely why referrals are so powerful (and why we will be getting back to them later in the book). Getting a referral from a mutual friend or colleague is a fast-pass into someone's social or professional "in-group."

When you are trying to establish a professional relationship, and you do not have any obvious in-group connections, pay attention for category overlap between you and your prospect, and look for opportunities to emphasize your shared connections.

If you do not currently have overlap, and you would like to, listen closely and try to pick up on some categories in which they consider themselves a member, especially those that sound interesting to you. When a prospect or customer opens up and shares a personal interest or group they belong to that resonates with you, even if it is not something you are currently pursuing, take advantage of the opportunity to inquire about it.

Showing authentic interest in something your prospect is personally vested in is a good way to begin making the shift from out-group to in-group. If you keep an open mind, you are likely to be able to find unique opportunities to form an in-group connection with someone with whom it might otherwise be hard to see something in common.

The more category connections you are able to make with a prospect, the more you are able to show your similarity and unity, and the more benefits of in-group membership you will realize. Not least of these is being more liked—the first step toward making a professional friend.

———

To recap our discussion of the behavioral dynamics of relationship building, people are lazy because of the law of least effort: effort comes at a cost, and reducing that cost maximizes efficiency. Often, however, it does so at the expense of rational thinking.

Adapting toward efficiency, humans evolved mental thought processes that hinged on the availability of an idea, rather than its rational merit, thus developing our minds' availability bias. Over millions of years of evolution, our minds have also developed two distinct modes of thought: System 1, our cost-effective autopilot and default mode of thought, and System 2, our "in case of emergency," highly rational, but cognitively expensive mode.

The law of least effort, availability bias, and two-system thinking form a behavioral trifecta that frequently manifests in the form of representativeness biases, including—and most important in the context of the sales cycle—the lazy ghosts of stereotyping and in-group bias.

Rather than attempting to disprove any negative preconceptions about you that may be lingering in your prospects' minds, connecting with the lazy ghosts—in order to be more liked—is all about finding ways to use what you know about similarity and representativeness to encourage those prospects to see past those small-minded preconceptions to the positives of building a relationship with you.

With this fundamental understanding of the behavioral dynamics that impact our relationship-building efforts, you will be empowered to take responsibility for a variety of the representative associations your prospects make of you.

We will now move on to a few tools that will help make sure your book's cover looks its best—to help your prospects see the version of you that is as easy as possible to accept, open up to, and like.

SHUT UP AND LISTEN

"We have two ears and one mouth so that we can listen twice as much as we speak."
—Epictetus

In my early twenties, I was an outside salesperson for a newswire distribution company. My territory covered a hodgepodge of southeastern and midwestern states, which I would visit with some regularity. Having spent my entire life in California—aside from the occasional family vacation somewhere else in the States—I did not grow up with an appreciation for the cultural differences between the major regions of the US. As anyone who has had occasion to spend extended periods of time in different parts of the US will attest, we may speak the same language, but we do not come from or perceive the same world.

One meeting I had with a Texas businessman stands out.

From the jump, the two of us blended together like oil and water. We literally had nothing in common. He was in his sixties and I was in my twenties. He looked like Boss Hogg from the Dukes of Hazzard, complete with white suit, bolo tie, and ten-gallon hat. I looked like a kid who had just graduated from college, with slicked-back hair and the most casual of business casual outfits.

He spoke with a classic Texas twang, his cadence slow and deliberate. I am and was a fast talker, generally anxious to get to the point. He wanted to talk about everything except what I was there to sell, which frustrated me; I kept trying to steer the conversation away from his personal interests toward the business at hand, which clearly frustrated him. The whole thing felt disjointed and unproductive. When our hour was up, he politely thanked me for making the trip and showed me the door.

Needless to say, we did not schedule a follow-up meeting, nor did we end up doing business together.

Looking back at this interaction, I realize now that I made one of the classic mistakes that I have warned you about above—continually trying to bring the focus back to me and my value proposition. However, amongst all the awkwardness of that meeting, what most stands out to me now is that I did not make any effort to listen and adjust toward that businessman. I see that as my biggest failure.

It would have really helped my twenty-something-year-old-self had I understood that people often see the world as revolving around them (lord knows I thought it revolved around me). We see ourselves as stars in a movie, and we feel as though life's spotlight is constantly shining down on us. There is even a name for this tendency: *the spotlight effect*. And, just like most actual movie stars, we are eager to discuss our movie with others, eager to share all the amazing details of our wonderful biopic masterpiece.

This little tidbit hides a relationship-building treasure. When meeting with a prospect or customer, remember: you are in their movie. They are the star of the show.

People find it inherently rewarding to talk about themselves and what they think. Studies show that sharing what is on our minds triggers the regions of our brains that are associated with motivation and reward.[60] Counterintuitively, this means that your prospects will develop a better impression of you the more you enable them to share with you—that is, the more you let them talk about themselves.

If you want your prospects and customers to like you better, all you have to do is provide them with the opportunity to share with you. Unfortunately, when it comes to listening, most salespeople are not so great.

As we have already discussed, most salespeople—my younger self included—assume that people want or need to hear about all the incredible value they are missing out on, all the wonderful things the salesperson could do for them. People hear Alec Baldwin's character in Glengarry Glen Ross[61] challenge the sales team to "always be closing" and assume that being a slick talker is what sales is all about.

But the thing is, sales is not about you.

You may *think* you have a tremendous value proposition that would be a perfect fit, but if you do not understand the specific things that are important to each individual prospect, you do not really *know*. You can only know if your value proposition is a good fit *after* you understand all those specific things that your prospect cares about. Without that understanding, you are just throwing things against the wall and hoping something sticks.

---

60   Diana I. Tamir and Jason P. Mitchell, "Disclosing Information about the Self Is Intrinsically Rewarding," *Proceedings of the National Academy of Sciences of the United States of America* 109, no. 21 (May 22): 8038–43.
61   Glengarry Glen Ross is a film depicting the desperation of a group of salespeople when the corporate office sends a trainer to motivate them, with Mr. Baldwin playing the role of trainer.

Most people are surprised to learn that the best salespeople are not the best talkers; the best salespeople are the best listeners.

The only way to understand someone is to listen to them. **Listening is the bridge between being an antagonist in the out-group and leveraging representativeness to connect with the lazy ghosts and become welcomed as part of the in-group.** Listening is how you pick up on category overlap and connections you might have with your prosects and customers. Listening is how you find similarity. Therefore, sales fundamentally begins with listening.

Although this truth flies under the radar in many sales cycle methodologies, it has been known for a long time.

- Dale Carnegie published *How to Win Friends and Influence People* in 1936, and among his "Six Ways to Make People Like You," he highlights, "Be a good listener. Encourage others to talk about themselves" as number four.[62]
- Habit number five of Stephen Covey's 1989 self-help masterpiece, *7 Habits of Highly Effective People*, is "Seek First to Understand. Then to Be Understood."[63]

These are two of the most highly regarded, best-selling, and most effective self-help books ever published, thanks in large part to the way they clearly illuminate many of life's truisms, including the importance of listening.

As a salesperson trying to understand how to make professional friends, it is vital that you step out of the shoes of the

---

62   Dale Carnegie, *How to Win Friends & Influence People* (New York: Simon & Schuster, 1936).
63   Stephen R. Covey, *The 7 Habits of Highly Effective People* (New York: Free Press, 1989).

antagonist and assist prospects in moving past their initial resistance to you by listening. There is no more important lesson to learn. Prospects buy from people they like, and they are much more apt to like people who—by listening— are able to recognize and highlight the ways in which they are similar.

In the early stages of relationship building, it is paramount to put away your pitch and just focus on the person in front of you. Listen to their story, their interests, their opinions, etc. Do not just hear and record the words they say. Do not just wait for your turn to talk; allow your responses and questions to be guided by what *they* choose to share. Show them that you are sincerely interested. Strive to see the world through their eyes. This is called *active listening*.

To be an active listener is to observe and recognize all aspects of the speaker's communication, including both verbal and nonverbal cues. Doing so enables the listener to better understand exactly what the speaker is trying to say. Thomas Gordon, who coined the term "active listening," says that "Active listening is certainly not complex. Listeners need only restate, in their own language, their impression of the expression of the sender...still, learning to do active listening well is a rather difficult task..."[64]

Contrary to what many salespeople and organizations believe, you do not have to be an expert to drive sales; you do not have to know everything about your prospect's role. Beyond demonstrating a high-level understanding of what someone does, it is often better *not* to know everything— to let curiosity be your guide.

People do not necessarily *like* experts. People like people

---

64   Thomas Gordon, *Leader Effectiveness Training: L. E. T.; Proven Skills for Leading Today's Business into Tomorrow* (New York: Berkley, 2001).

who show an interest in what they think and do, people who seek to understand them. Feeling understood will lower your prospect's guard, which will free them to open up and trust you, which will empower you to help them. Active listening is how you show your prospects and customers you understand.

When you are first getting to know someone, what *you* think, no matter how insightful or brilliant, does not matter until you are able to demonstrate that you understand and appreciate what *they* think. **When you are trying to develop a relationship and establish trust, you need to let go of your pitch.** You need to let go of trying to "sell" to your prospects. Instead, it is time to take their perspective. You need to put yourself in their shoes.

Fortunately for us, behavioral science suggests a few specific ways you can do just that.

CHANGING GEARS

"Be water, my friend."
—Bruce Lee

In the 1970s, Richard Bandler and John Grinder developed an approach to communication and personal development based on the connection between neurological processes, language, and behavior patterns. They called their approach Neuro-Linguistic Programming (NLP) and claimed that manipulation of these three variables was the key to eliminating a variety of psychological problems—including phobias, depression, and various learning disorders—as well as achieving your life's goals.

NLP bills itself as the "science of success" and the "art of communication." Although the scientific claims made by NLP are controversial and often do not stand up to the rigor of scientific testing, the guidance NLP gives in the art of communication has much to offer salespeople interested in managing the representativeness associations that prospects and customers will be making of them.

NLP was an early adopter of the importance of nonverbal communication. One of the primary tenets of NLP's art of communication is that the meaning of communication is the response you get. The program argues that body language and expressed tonality are the most important part of communication in terms of generating a response. This point is supported by research done by Albert Mehrabian at UCLA in the 1960s, where he reported that only 7% of communication is verbal, while body language and tonality account for 55% and 38% of communication, respectively.[65]

According to NLP, relationships are established and solidified when we are able to speak the same language as someone else. In this case, to "speak the same language" is not so much about using the same words that person does, but about matching and mirroring their body language and tonality.

Per Mehrabian's research, these two "languages" are more important than the actual content of the conversation.

Matching and *mirroring*—the blocking and tackling of body language and tonality—are techniques that salespeople can use to establish better relationships with their prospects and customers. Mirroring and matching are two tools that are key to accessing the emotional 70% of

---

65   Albert Mehrabian, *Silent Messages: Implicit Communication of Emotions and Attitudes* (Belmont, CA: Wadsworth, 1971).

decision-making, providing another path to liking through similarity in movement and tone.

Strictly defined, matching is generally expressing yourself in the same way as another person, while mirroring is to move in sync with another person, as though you were a mirror reflection of them. Acting classes often play mirroring games as an intentional way to bring awareness to body movement and to get actors in sync with one another.

More loosely defined, mirroring and matching are all about meeting another person where they are and adjusting toward them.

In preparation for the meeting with the Texas businessman all those years ago, I gave no consideration to who this person I would be meeting with was and what he might be interested in; all of my preparation was to do with the service I was selling.

We had spoken on the phone briefly prior to our meeting, yet I paid little attention to how he spoke or what he spoke about. During our meeting, I made no effort to slow down my pace, nor did I express anything beyond superficial interest in what he wanted to talk about. On top of that, at that time in my life I can remember consciously choosing to dress as casually as was acceptable for my workplace, which I now know was actively disregarding the expectations of the prospects I met with.

There is no way of knowing, had I been more attentive in adjusting toward him, whether I would have earned his business or not. Even if I had been more aware of mirroring and matching back then, I still might not have been able to bridge a significant generation gap, and I definitely would not have shown up in a bolo tie and ten-gallon hat. But that is not the point.

The point is that I never even gave him the chance to open up to me. Rather than actively listening and looking for some way to connect with him, which could have been done by at least matching his body language and tone, I was too focused on pitching all the great aspects of the service I was selling, skipping over the emotional aspects of relationship building. I did not try to find similarities with him at any level; instead, I lobbed the features, advantages, and benefits of my service at him in the hope that something would stick. Just about the only thing I was successful in doing was allowing the lazy ghosts to place me squarely outside all of his in-groups and reinforce his view of me as just another sales antagonist.

If you are interested in establishing and building rapport with your prospects while making a crucial first impression, pay attention to their body language and tonality cues and adjust toward them.

To assist you in your efforts to actively listen and mirror and match your prospects, there are five key body language and tonality cues to look out for. All you have to remember is that adjusting toward your prospects is about learning how to change GEARS.[66]

---

66   The mnemonic device is mine (you're welcome), but the concepts are taken directly from NLP research.

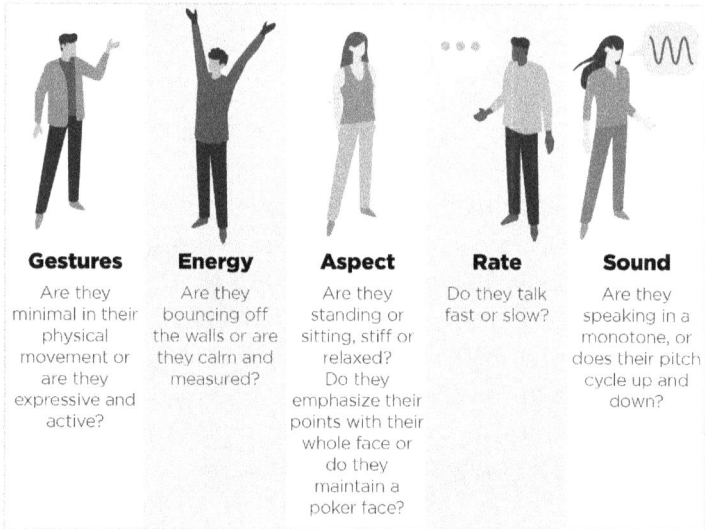

Gestures	Energy	Aspect	Rate	Sound
Are they minimal in their physical movement or are they expressive and active?	Are they bouncing off the walls or are they calm and measured?	Are they standing or sitting, stiff or relaxed? Do they emphasize their points with their whole face or do they maintain a poker face?	Do they talk fast or slow?	Are they speaking in a monotone, or does their pitch cycle up and down?

Keep in mind, mirroring and matching are not about superficial mimicry or imitation. They are not about trying to trick or hypnotize your prospects. Rather, they are about recognizing and adjusting to more than just the words that are being exchanged.

Mirroring and matching are effective foils for the lazy ghosts, helping you connect with them, but they are not cure-alls. Rather—like all of the strategies in this book—mirroring and matching help increase the odds that you will make a connection and earn the opportunity to win your prospect's business.

KNOW YOUR AUDIENCE

"Positioning is the single largest influence on the buying decision."
—Geoffrey A. Moore

If you are actively listening and changing GEARS appropriately, a picture of the type of person you are speaking with will begin to come into focus—what they value, what groups they see themselves as a part of, what kind of perspective they bring to their business, and more.

Finding common ground with your prospects and customers is only the tip of the iceberg. The more detailed and well-rounded your picture of the person in front of you, the more likely you are to connect with them—and the better you will be able to understand *how* to sell to them.

One of the best tools to assist you in your efforts to actively listen and change GEARS is the buyer-type chart, which is based on research done in the 1940s by Neal Gross and Bryce Ryan on the adoption of newly developed hybrid seed corn among Iowa farmers.[67]

In their work, Gross and Ryan identified five types of adopters (aka buyers). These five types have withstood the test of time and remain as relevant to the sales cycle today as they were all those years ago in Iowa.[68] This chart, based on Ryan and Gross's insights, offers high-level guidance that will help frame your value proposition to optimally speak to the buyer sitting in front of you. We will talk more about framing as a concept in the next chapter, but for now, all you need to know is that this chart can be a powerful resource that will help you speak in terms that will resonate with your prospects and customers.

---

67   Bryce Ryan and Neal Gross, "Acceptance and Diffusion of Hybrid Corn Seed in Two Iowa Communities," *Research Bulletin (Iowa Agriculture and Home Economics Experiment Station)* 29, no. 372 (1950): 661–708.

68   The five types were popularized by Geoffrey A. Moore's *Crossing the Chasm: Marketing and Selling High-Tech Products to Mainstream Customers* (New York: Harper Business Essentials, 1991).

	They want...	They buy...	Sell them...
The **Innovator**	to be on the cutting edge	trials/tests	innovation
The **Early Adopter**	to get in early	customization	differentiation
The **Early Majority**	to solve problems	total solutions	experience in solving similar problems
The **Late Majority**	to not be left behind	proven industry standards	return on investment
The **Laggard**	the status que	enhancing/ extending existing systems	investment protection

To find out where your prospect or customer stands, listen for the way they talk about what they like or want in a product or service. What keywords are they using? Do they speak of "solving problems"? Or are they more interested in being on "the cutting edge"? These cues will indicate which type of buyer you are working with. Once you identify their type, simply move from left to right in the chart for guidance regarding what they buy and what—and *how*—you should sell. Simple.

Subsequent analysis of Ryan and Gross's work illuminates the relative concentrations of each type...

- ~68% of buyers are evenly split between the early majority and late majority
- ~30% are evenly split between laggards and early adopter categories
- a mere ~2% are recognized as innovators[69]

...which means that most of your time will be spent either with folks in the early or late majority. So make sure your referrals are strong and your ROI metrics are sharp!

Of course, this is not a magic trick, and there is no promise of guaranteed success if you use this chart. **Instead, consistent application of the high-level insights provided by this chart will help you deliver messages your prospects are receptive to and demonstrate to them that you have been listening to them.** Prospects who feel that you understand them will be more inclined to like you, ultimately increasing the odds that you will be able to build a strong relationship with them.

BONUS: MOOD CONGRUENCE

Being able to read the room is a valuable skill for a salesperson to possess. Specifically, to *read the room* is to be in tune with the mood of the individuals around you. People's actions are generally congruent with their mood; they tend to respond to ideas in ways that align with how they are currently feeling. This is what it means to have mood congruence.

Salespeople need to learn to read the room in order to recognize those times when their prospects are open to receiving their message.

---

69   Everett M. Rogers, *Diffusions of Innovations*, 3rd ed. (New York: Free Press, 1983).

From the moment a meeting or presentation begins, take note of your prospect's mood and the general vibe in the room or on the phone. Are they in a bad mood? Are they distracted? Are they especially busy? Are they exhibiting open body language? Do they ask questions about and show interest in what you are talking about? This is how you tune in to the mood: how you read the room.

In effect, to recognize mood congruence and adjust accordingly is to double down on active listening.

Always be aware of your surroundings and the people in them before you go about trying to sell anybody anything. If your prospect is less than open and engaged, do yourself a favor and save your pitch for another day. Trust and believe that, if you learn to read the room, the right opportunity to influence others will present itself.

———

We have taken a long walk to make a pretty simple point: when deciding whom to establish business partnerships with, people do not necessarily prioritize what is right or rational. Rather, people react to what is most readily accessible in their minds. Often, those are first impressions and stereotypes generated by fast and frugal System 1 thinking—which predispose prospects to think of salespeople as antagonists.

Relationship building is all about treating the people before you as professional friends—human beings first and customers second—and seeking out similarities with them so that they will be more inclined to like you, trust you, and, in turn, buy from you.

Think of the techniques we have discussed in this chapter as the judo moves of our behavioral approach to relationship building: rather than pushing back against the snap judgements prospects and customers will make about you, understand how these instinctual reactions work and use them to your advantage when possible.

Be proactive about creating impressions, highlighting similarities, and adjusting your body language and tone to increase the odds that you will be liked. This is what being "a bit more deliberate" in making professional friends is all about. Do not make the mistake of leading with logic and reason. Instead, take the path of least resistance and actively listen, doing your best to understand their point of view, so that you may connect with the lazy ghosts in their mental machinery and help them open up to you.

In time, you will feel yourself migrating past superficial meetings to a place where prospects and customers are actively seeking your advice. This is exactly where you want to be.

Next, let's take a look at what they do when they actually start thinking about buying from you. As it turns out, there are plenty of ghosts in the machine that haunt that part of the process as well.

CHANGING

Every single human being on the planet, including you and me, has had the experience of sticking with something they already have or do—whether it be clothes, tools, a specific morning routine or a favorite set of homecooked meals—for no better reason than it is what we have always done. This has been scientifically documented,[70] but we need look no further than our own living rooms to understand that it is true.

Like most Americans, I have spent an inordinate amount of my life watching television. It was my favorite babysitter when I was young, my favorite distraction from homework when I was in school, and it remains my favorite way to keep up with popular culture.

Ever since it became commonplace after World War II, TV has been a favorite pastime of Americans of all ages.

70   William Samuelson and Richard Zeckhauser, "Status Quo Bias in Decision Making," *Journal of Risk and Uncertainty* 1, no. 1 (March 1988): 7–59.

Our collective passion for television accelerated with the commercial introduction of cable in the eighties, making it the centerpiece in satisfying our ever-growing thirst for in-home entertainment. Evolving over the next forty years into a 700-channel behemoth, cable solidified its position as the go-to source for in-home entertainment.

Then we met the internet.[71]

At first, the internet was a text-heavy medium, dominated by chat rooms and web pages that resembled book pages more than they did movies—not much of a threat to the reign of TV. But over time, as technological capabilities advanced and people demanded more than just chat rooms and blocks of electronic text, the internet started to flex its entertainment muscles.

Today, through the magic of streaming, the internet directly competes with cable TV for all of our entertainment needs. Cable TV may offer 700+ channels to choose from, but streaming delivers a mind-bending, practically limitless variety of choices, including much of cable's programming. Differences in picture quality and the speed of delivery between the two are now negligible. And, perhaps most importantly, the cost difference is also negligible—if not significantly in favor of streaming online.[72]

In fact, many people have already decided that streaming is superior to cable. The number of "cord-cutters"[73] who

---

71   Satellite TV will be ignored for purposes of simplifying this discussion.

72   Per DecisionData, on average, cable TV costs $217.42 per month; monthly internet service costs around $60 per month, plus the cost of a streaming internet service (e.g. Hulu), which costs $6 to $61 per month. See "REPORT: The Average Cable Bill Now Exceeds All Other Household Utility Bills Combined," DecisionData, June 22, 2020, https://decisiondata.org/news/report-the-average-cable-bill-now-exceeds-all-other-household-utility-bills-combined/; Eli Blumenthal, "Internet Bill Too High? Here's How to Save," USA Today, January 8, 2018; and Rachel Morgan Cautero, "What's the Average Cost of Video Streaming Services?" Balance, March 10, 2020.

73   It's ironic that replacing one type of cord (cable TV) with another (in-

have made the switch from cable to streaming services has steadily increased ever since internet TV became a practical reality around 2010. As of 2020, more people now subscribe to a streaming service (69%) than subscribe to cable TV (65%).[74]

But the question I want to ask is this: why haven't more people already made the switch—starting with me?

DECIDING NOT TO DECIDE

I have been threatening to cut the cord for at least ten years, but I have never really gotten close to doing it. For one, streaming feels more complicated. Cable is simple: you pay a single monthly price and you get 700+ channels. Streaming requires at least two separate services to replicate the cable experience—internet service plus a streaming service—not to mention the rabbit hole of additional options that are available. To date, when push has come to shove, I have not felt like putting the time and effort into figuring it out; it is just not a priority. (Naturally: I am lazy, just like everyone else.)

Secondly, I am afraid I will lose access to something when and if I cut the cord. Live sports and local news jump to mind. I have never really experienced in-home streaming as a primary entertainment medium and am unsure what it would actually be like. It is probably a safe bet that I would not miss much, if anything, but I do not know for sure—and that has been enough to keep me tuning in to the television as I have always done.

ternet wires) would identify one as a "cord-cutter," when really you are just a cord-switcher, but I digress.

74   Per Starry, an internet service provider; that these figures taken together are >100% reflects the fact that there are people who subscribe to both. See "Cord Cutting on the Rise: 9 Stats and Trends," *The Download* (blog), Starry, December 11, 2019, https://starry.com/blog/inside-the-internet/cord-cutting-stats-and-trends.

Every time I start thinking about cutting the cord, where does that thought process lead? The simple answer is that it leads to indecision. I end up pushing the choice to later; I end up deciding not to decide.

Now that we have made it to the changing phase of the sales cycle, your prospect is actively considering making a change from whatever it is they are currently doing. This is right where you want to be. So at this point, it is time to explore the many ghosts that stymie efficient decision-making in all of us, including professional decision-makers.

A major obstacle many sales professionals may encounter at this stage is prospects kicking the can down the road, unsure whether to take the plunge and buy a new product or service. Instead of making a choice, decision-makers often decide not to decide. According to the 2014 Sales Benchmark Index, 58% of opportunities end up in "no decision."

Of course, for the salesperson, a lack of decision at this stage is pretty much the same as a no.

For me—and likely for most of the 65% of consumers who are also still tied to cable—the fear of losing some kind of access, even if we are not sure what it would be, when combined with the perceived effort it would take to switch providers, overwhelms any logical reasons there might be to switch from cable to streaming. This emotionally driven resistance to change mirrors the resistance that salespeople receive from their customers when presenting their products and services.

Most salespeople have been trained to attack the resistance they get from prospects at this stage head-on, with all manner of rational arguments and selling points.

Unfortunately, few things could be less effective in trying to achieve success.

To begin to learn how to affect change in our prospects and customers in the most effective way possible, we have to understand why people decide not to decide. And to do that, we have to understand how the human brain has evolved to think about changing.

THINKING ABOUT IT

> *"Thinking is the hardest work there is, which is the probable reason why so few engage in it."*
> *—Henry Ford*

Let's take a moment a recap our sales cycle journey thus far.

We began by setting ourselves up for prospecting success by playing the numbers game to get a foot in the door, avoiding the deceitful ghosts in our own minds along the way. Once we had crafted a strong prospecting process and were generating leads, we then focused on establishing and building strong relationships, rather than pitching our products and services—actively listening in order to connect with the busy and lazy ghosts in the minds of our prospects and customers.

Now our hard work is starting to pay off, and those prospects are actively considering working with us. At last we are beginning to see that they are open to making a change.

Changing is where the fun really begins—and it marks the beginning of what most consider "selling."

Many people, especially those on the outside looking in, view the sales profession as an exceptional function reserved for those with outgrown personalities and an unsatiable desire to compete. Further, many view "selling" as a single act, wherein, through power of will and magic of words, the salesperson changes another person's mind and talks them into a deal in one fell swoop.

Putting aside the disregard this perception has for the importance of the prospecting and relationship-building aspects of being a successful salesperson, a view of "selling" as a single act is also fundamentally flawed.

The first thing we need to understand is that what most consider selling can be cleanly separated into two sequential components: changing (or affecting change) and negotiating.

In the next two chapters we will break down these component parts of selling and come out with a better understanding of what inhibits success at each stage, using this understanding to unlock the keys to success—both in our attempts to affect change and, finally, as we meet our prospects at the negotiating table.

First, we will dive into changing.

A salesperson's job, fundamentally, is to try to get prospects and customers to do one of two things:

1. Switch products or services
2. Embrace new products or services that they are
   not currently utilizing

In either case, change is what is for sale. If the salesperson succeeds, the prospect buys something, and a change is made. If the salesperson fails, no change is made, and the prospect goes on doing the same thing they were already doing, having decided not to decide.

In order to successfully make a sale, you will have to do one of the hardest things there is to do: influence another human being to change their mind.

Change is not an easy thing. Everyone struggles with changing their mind, no matter how trivial or critical the circumstances. This is such a fundamental aspect of human nature that, when attempting to affect change in the minds of your prospects, before you can get around to answering the question "why choose us," you must be ready to tackle a much more basic question: "why change at all?"

As we have already discussed, salespeople are often too eager to share all the wonderful things their products or services could do for their customers. In addition to side-tracking a salesperson's efforts in the relationship-building stage, being overeager to launch into selling points also leads salespeople to prematurely skip over the "why change" part altogether.

Be warned: if you lead your pitch with all the wonderful features, advantages, and benefits of your product or service before your prospect recognizes a clear reason to change in the first place, your pitch will fall on deaf ears.

Do not make this mistake. Do not leave your active listening behind in the relationship-building stage. Keep listening actively and stay focused on clearly understanding your prospect's response to the question "why change?" before you attempt to pitch "why choose us."

This may be where you spend the majority of your time in the sales cycle, because getting someone to open up and honestly consider the very *idea* of changing can be the hardest sale to make.

Think back to the last time you debated the merits of something with a friend or colleague, with each of you earnestly trying to win the other over to their way of thinking. Replay the interaction in your mind. Recall how the points you made landed. What was the other person's response like? What was your response to their points?

If your family and friends' debates—political or otherwise—are anything like the debates I have with my family and friends, they usually kick off with someone sharing a thought, idea, or opinion, which is immediately followed by someone explaining why that thought is wrong and stupid before launching into a seemingly rehearsed list of reasons why. From there, a back-and-forth, loosely guided by the alternate sharing and rebutting of specific data points, ensues. All the while, the combatants dig their heels in further and further, alienating everyone else who is not actively engaged in the debate, and very little, if any, change occurs.

Sound familiar?

Does anyone ever "win" these arguments? Anyone ever say, "Gee. You are so right and I was so wrong. Thank you for changing my mind"?

Of course not.

In the 1936 bestseller that helped create the self-help book industry, *How to Win Friends and Influence People*, Dale Carnegie shares this little pearl of wisdom: "The only way to get the best of an argument is to avoid it."[75] Those are wise words. Although I hesitate to say never, well, you will

---

75   Dale Carnegie, *How to Win Friends & Influence People* (New York: Simon & Schuster, 1936).

almost never change someone's mind by arguing with them about facts and figures. This is true whether you are debating the finer points of foreign policy with a friend or discussing the merits of implementing a new software system with a prospect.

And you had better not disparage the other person's opinion, no matter how much you might disagree. "Show respect for the other person's opinions," Mr. Carnegie writes. "Never say 'You're wrong.'"[76]

People *really* do not like to be wrong. One of the primary reasons people are less than enthusiastic about changing their minds is the idea that change must be an implicit acknowledgement that a previous decision or choice was wrong. Your prospects are likely to resist the idea that their current situation could be made better by your product or service simply because that would mean their previous decision to go with their current product or service was a bad one.

This is precisely why it is often easier to convince a prospect to make a change when there is a turnover of decision-makers. The outgoing decision-makers were likely married to the way things were and therefore resistant to change for fear of admitting a previous decision was wrong. Conversely, the new decision-maker is free to make a change without having to wrestle with acknowledging the wrongness of a previous decision because it was not theirs. This can make them more open—relatively, anyway—to making a change.

The other major reason why humans resist change—and the one we will focus on in this chapter—is because we actually have to think about it.

---

76   Carnegie, *How to Win Friends.*

Whether we are considering cutting the cord or switching accounting firms, thinking is hard, and we human beings will avoid it if at all possible. As we learned in the last chapter, human minds are biased toward "fast and frugal" thought patterns that make mental life easier. People prefer ideas that confirm rather than conflict with their pre-linked mental associations simply because confirmation is easier to process

From the perspective of behavioral science, attempting to change someone's mind with rational arguments is really an attempt to get them to actively resist an association that already exists in their mind—such as an established relationship with a current product or service provider— by deliberately and effortfully weighing the pros and cons of the new practice versus the old one.

To put these in terms we discussed in the previous chapter, even if we are trying to engage with our prospects' rational thought processes—their System 2 thinking—our arguments will be resisted by the availability bias, which gives human minds a natural tendency to assume that any pre-existing associations are the most important. Essentially, trying to get people to change their minds via rational arguments is forcing them to do the most mental work possible, all while suggesting that their original decision was wrong—not a great combo!

Given a choice, people would much rather stay on autopilot than do the heavy lifting of having to think about a decision. Staying on System 1's comfortable autopilot is the path of least, or at least less, resistance. Unfortunately for the salesperson, the path of least resistance does not drive sales.

What also does not drive sales is the approach to changing minds taken by traditional sales training.

Most sales training approaches the process of changing minds from a rational perspective, speaking only to system 2 strategies while disregarding both the effort required to be rational and the natural human distaste for questioning a past decision.

Salespeople are generally taught that, when pursuing a potential purchase, companies move through their collective decision-making process in sequential phases[77] that look something like this:

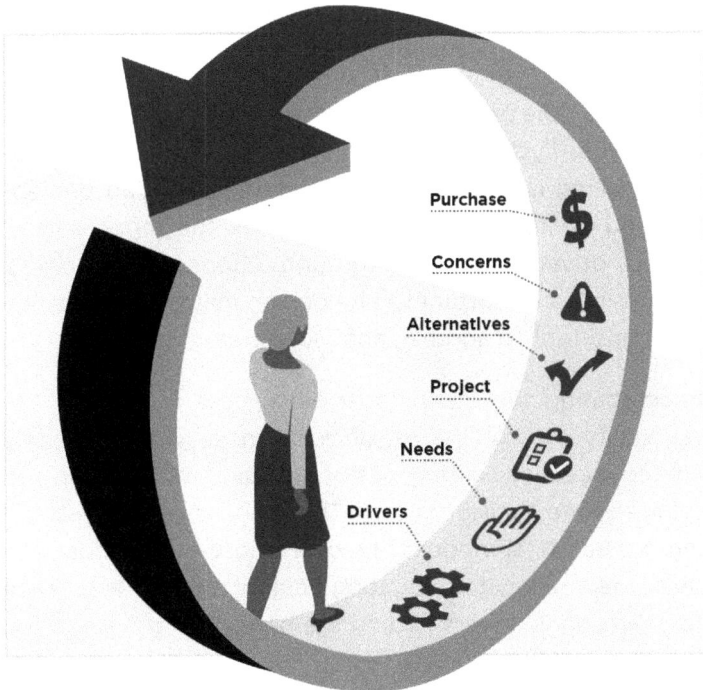

Purchase

Concerns

Alternatives

Project

Needs

Drivers

---

77   While there are various sales methodologies that do *not* teach the buying cycle as a strictly linear process, arguing that there is some degree of cycling back and forth between phases, nearly all methodologies maintain that the high-level process of the buying cycle will generally flow in a start-to-finish fashion, beginning with drivers and ending with a purchase.

This is known as the buying cycle—it is the way decision-making about a purchase is "supposed" to go. These steps are generally useful and informative, and salespeople would do well to understand this construct, but this version of the buying cycle is missing a critical component: the human beings that do the decision-making.

A straight walk through the buying cycle may represent theoretical "best practice," but, as we have learned at every step in our journey through the sales cycle thus far, people are not very good at rationally, robotically following "best practice." Our inevitable deviations from linear pathways such as the buying cycle are accounted for by the ghosts in the machine, all those biases and cognitive shortcuts that impact how human beings think.

Remember, the people actually making the decisions within the buying cycle are just regular people, and their decision-making is haunted by mismatches between perception and reality. They will invariably view the importance of various drivers and needs through differing perspectives. What is most important to one person may be significantly less important to another, and vice versa.

Exacerbating these inevitable differences of opinion, the rationality of professional decision-making is necessarily limited–because shifting out of autopilot and stopping to think about a decision is hard. Therefore, rather than studying a theoretical model of how decisions are supposed to be made, the key to mitigating your customers' resistance to changing is understanding the behavioral drivers of the decision-making process.

When it comes to decision-making, it turns out that *how* people think about changing has a far more profound effect on the outcome than the sequential steps that are supposed to unfold. In order to understand how a sales-person can be best positioned to affect change, we will now take a deep dive into the various irrational—yet evo-lutionarily effective—thought processes that the human mind goes through in the process of trying to decide.

FEAR OF THE UNKNOWN

"The oldest and strongest emotion of mankind is
fear, and the oldest and strongest kind of fear
is fear of the unknown."
—H.P. Lovecraft

In a 2016 study,[78] groups of participants were presented with a series of choices between two rocks, along with varying probabilities of receiving an electric shock to their hand based on their selection. The probability they would receive a shock varied from 50% to 100%. The experiment was designed to measure participants' stress responses based on various probabilities of being shocked.

Rather counterintuitively, the experiment demonstrated that having a 50% chance of being shocked generated the greatest stress response from participants. The research-ers concluded that participants' stress responses were pre-dicted, not by the anticipation of pain, but by the level of irreducible uncertainty[79] they experienced. In other words, the circumstance with the highest level of uncertainty generated the highest level of stress. A 50% chance of a shock—peak irreducible uncertainty—was more stressful to study participants than knowing with 100% certainty that a shock was coming.

---

78 De Berker et al., "Computations of Uncertainty Mediate Acute Stress Responses in Humans," Nature Communications 7, no. 10996 (2016).
79 The essential randomness of a given environment.

Think about that. It is more stressful to be uncertain whether or not you will experience pain than it is to know for certain that pain is coming.

This finding cuts right to the heart of the challenges salespeople face when our prospects are considering changing products or services—a set of challenges created by the fearful ghosts, which we will be meeting in a moment.

We will be discussing uncertainty quite a bit in this chapter, so let's level-set on exactly what we mean when we say uncertainty or when we talk about uncertain events. Uncertainty refers to situations involving imperfect or unknown information, and it generally applies to predictions of future events. Most importantly, when people make choices that will impact the future—like a prospect deciding to switch vendors—there will *always* be some degree of uncertainty.

People may not like being wrong, but they are absolutely petrified of uncertainty. **When human beings are confronted with a choice between the known and unknown, the fearful ghosts in the machine step forward and encourage them to stick with the thing they already know—whether by outright saying no to new options or by deciding not to decide.**

Nowhere is this truer than in the world of financial services. Having spent the last ten years of my career selling various types of credit products, I can confidently say that unseating a current financial services provider is among the most challenging changes a salesperson can try to affect.

Whether a company has a love or hate relationship with their financial services provider, they can still feel relatively certain about what they are getting. The thought of changing providers—inviting another bank or financial institution in to go through the exhaustive and disruptive process of underwriting, possibly screwing up the management of their money—might be the most terrifying thought a company's financial executives could have.

From the perspective of behavioral science, uncertainty makes us anxious and fearful because it disrupts our System 1 autopilot, shifting our System 2 thinking into gear.

For example, if we know for certain that pain of some kind is coming, then we are able to stay on autopilot, because there is nothing we can do about it. But when we are unsure whether or not we will experience pain, we have to think about it using our higher-level cognitive facilities.

Jill Stoddard, clinical psychologist and author of *Be Mighty*, a book about managing anxiety, explains that "anxiety and discomfort are products of evolution. Anxious early humans who avoided uncertainty had a survival advantage."[80] Those early humans who were more motivated to avoid uncertain circumstances had a greater likelihood of survival than those who were less diligent about avoiding uncertainty—which is precisely how natural selection works.

Imagine a group of our ancestors starring in a horror movie. Those who ran from the mysterious noise in the distance—the anxious ones—would definitely have a greater chance of surviving. Those who were motivated to investigate—the brave ones—would be much more likely to get killed by whatever form Freddy, Jason, or the Babadook took way back then.

Uncertainty presents an even greater challenge to people in the modern world, accustomed as we are to all of our

---

80   Yael Schonbrun and Barry Schwartz, "How Practical Wisdom Helps Us Cope with Radical Uncertainty," *Behavioral Scientist*, August 31, 2020.

instant-gratification trappings. As Stoddard tells us: "If you want the answer to any question, just ask your device. If you want to know whether a restaurant, product, or service will meet your expectations, just go to your favorite search engine."[81]

Because modern technology has given us ways to eliminate or mitigate so many of life's day-to-day uncertainties, we may be less able to deal with the uncertainties that remain; essentially, we are out of practice, and our dealing-with-uncertainty-muscles have atrophied.

Enter COVID-19.

As I write, the world is suffering through the worst global pandemic since the Spanish flu. COVID-19 has flipped the world upside down, forcing people to distance from one another while attempting to find a new normal. As of July 2021, one hundred ninety-six million people have been infected with COVID-19 and four million have died. It is anyone's guess how this current pandemic will further unfold and eventually come to an end.

There are those who think COVID-19 is not a big deal and the world's political institutions are dramatically overreacting, crushing economies and ruining lives. They believe that the world should basically go back to normal, convinced that this will all blow over.

On the other hand, there are those who see the current pandemic as a very real threat to the health and safety of all, especially those in vulnerable populations. These folks believe that political institutions are not taking it seriously enough, and that is ruining lives. They believe that wearing masks, social distancing and sheltering in place are nonnegotiable moral imperatives.

---

81   Schonbrun and Schwartz, "How Practical Wisdom Helps Us Cope."

The biggest problem we all have is that nobody *knows* who is right.

At present, just about the only thing we do know regarding COVID-19 with any level of certainty is how awfully *uncertain* we are about what needs to be done and just how bad the virus is. From a behavioral science perspective, the uncertainty surrounding COVID-19 is the most challenging aspect of the pandemic.

People have always yearned for certainty in a world that offers only degrees of possibility. As Amos Tversky put it, "Man is a deterministic device thrown into a probabilistic universe."[82] Uncertainty—*not knowing*—has a profound impact on how human beings think, how we perceive the world around us.

Uncertainty brings fearful thoughts that would otherwise lie dormant to the forefront of our minds, and these fearful thoughts can drive irrational behavior.

Fear of uncertainty about the future will always haunt humanity. It is deeply engrained in our psyche, because uncertainty was risky for our hunter-gatherer ancestors in a life-and-death kind of way. And when it comes to modern-day sales, the fear of uncertainty rears its ugly head every time your prospects and customers have to make a decision.

These fears have a tangible effect on the sales cycle. Though the professional decision-maker may have some confidence around the likely outcome of their choices, they can never really know what is going to happen until well after the decision is made. Take the decision to hire or fire someone, for example. This is among the most crucial

82   Michael Lewis, *The Undoing Project: A Friendship That Changed Our Minds* (New York: W. W. Norton, 2016), 197.

decisions made in the professional setting, and there are usually robust debates on the merits of hiring or firing—all without anyone being able to predict the outcome and therefore definitively stake a claim to the "right" answer. The decision to expand or reduce the size of your team is anything but black and white. The reason is uncertainty.

When it comes to the sales cycle, even if you are successful in establishing a connection with your prospect, as we discussed in the previous chapter, your services still represent an unknown quantity if that person has never worked with you before. Even if your company is broadly known in the marketplace—through longevity or sheer force of marketing—it still represents a perceived risk. And even if your company's products operate within a highly commoditized and mature industry, they will still trigger your prospect's fear of the unknown if said prospect has never had the occasion to actually use your version of them.

Breaking through the fear of the unknown is the single most challenging obstacle you will face throughout the sales cycle.

Most salespeople consider their primary competition to be the shop down the street that does the same thing they do. And to say that salespeople need be familiar with their competition is to state the obvious. Having knowledge of the companies you compete with, and how to position your products and services relative to theirs, is Sales 101. That said, those companies are not your primary competition.

The one thing that most often stands in the way of affecting change and winning new business—your fiercest competition—is the fear of uncertainty that haunts professional decision-making. Uncertainty is why 58% of sales opportunities end in no decision. As often as not (and probably more often), you will lose to an incumbent product or service simply because people feel that the devil they know is better than the one they do not.

The purely rational model of decision-making, which most traditional sales training methodologies take as a given, misses the mark when it comes to how decision-makers actually respond to uncertain circumstances. When considering a change, your prospects are always going to perceive degrees of uncertainty, which necessarily means that their response will deviate from the cookie-cutter version of decision-making found in most sales training systems.

Disregarding the impact that fear of uncertainty has on decision-making, and assuming your prospects and customers are perfectly rational, is a recipe for failure. What salespeople need is a new perspective that embraces the uncertainty their prospects feel when making decisions.

Enter *prospect theory*, behavioral science's answer to rational choice theory and the perfectly rational decision-maker.

PROSPECT THEORY

Prospect theory—an analysis of decision-making behavior under circumstances of uncertainty and risk—is one of the foundational concepts of behavioral science. Developed by Daniel Kahneman and Amos Tversky in 1979—and earning Kahneman the Nobel Prize in 2002—prospect theory challenges the rational choice theory assumption of the rational, objective pursuit of expected utility.

Prospect theory illustrates that people are generally loss-averse, preferring to avoid losses over the pursuit of equivalent gains. Taking a bit of a logical leap—and sparing you many mind-numbing details—what prospect theory really proves is that people anchor their decision-making to a reference point rather than making decisions from an objective point of view.

Prospect theory outlines a two-step decision-making process:

- *Editing—Potential choices are ranked and compared with a reference point, which is often tied to the individual's current circumstances.*

- *Evaluation—Relative to the reference point, potential choices are then considered either more or less valuable, which is further influenced by their proximity to the reference point.*

In layman's terms, people make decisions based on the potential gains or losses relative to their specific situation rather than in absolute or objective terms.

For example, a person with no money, whose reference point is being broke, will be eager to make a decision that would earn them $100. However, a decision to earn an extra $100, even though it is the exact same amount of money, would not do much for a millionaire, whose reference point is being rich.

Therefore, human beings are guided by the impact of relative gains and losses—not by absolute prospects of wealth and utility—and rational choice theory is fundamentally flawed because utility depends on context.

We do not need to be experts in the mathematical gymnastics that illustrate prospect theory's superiority to rational choice theory to recognize that its central tenets provide us with a more realistic view of decision-making in the context of uncertainty.

The existence and influence of reference points is the key insight here. Reference points provide the perception of certainty, of which decision-makers are very fond indeed.

Using my cable TV versus online streaming example: cable TV is my reference point. I am certain of what I will receive from my cable TV service. From this reference point, any decision to change I may make in the future will necessarily present me with less certainty. That is, a decision to change would *create* uncertainty. Always. And, just like the decision-makers you will cross paths with, I enjoy my certainty; very, very much. The relative certainty of reference points gives root to fear of loss, drives preference for the status quo in comparison to any new or untested option, and motivates the search for information that confirms pre-established beliefs. Say hello to the fearful ghosts—*loss aversion*, *the status quo bias*, and *confirmation bias*. You will be seeing a lot of them, because they are arguably the three most significant hurdles salespeople face when trying to affect change.

LOSS AVERSION

As we just discussed, one of the main things that frightens people about uncertainty is the possibility of a loss. And, in general, people behave in ways that minimize their losses.

More specifically, people tend to prefer avoiding losses to acquiring equivalent gains. Some studies suggest that losses are up to *twice* as powerful as gains in our mental calculus. In this light, we can see part of why uncertainty about outcomes is such a big deal.

Daniel Kahneman punctuates this phenomenon using a simple bet based on the flip of a coin, with a slight twist.

The bet is over a single flip. If the coin lands tails-up, you owe $10. He then asks you how much you would have to win if the coin lands heads-up to take the bet. Most people will not take the bet if they only stand to win $10, that is, the same amount they risk losing.

In fact, Kahneman has found that most people require more than $20 in winnings before they take the bet, even though the odds of winning and losing are identical. Further, Kahneman has found that the same two-to-one payoff ratio is required whether the amount is small, like $10, or large, like $10,000.[83]

Loss aversion is a powerful manifestation of our fear of uncertainty, and it brings those otherwise dormant, fearful thoughts to the forefront of our minds, affecting how we behave when we believe we stand to lose something. In *Thinking, Fast and Slow*, Kahneman writes, "The concept of loss aversion is certainly the most significant contribution of psychology to behavioral economics."[84] This is high praise from one of behavioral science's founding fathers.

Given the profound influence that loss aversion has on decision-making, there are three specific effects of this fearful ghost that salespeople need to be aware of when trying to affect change. You could consider these effects to be loss aversion ghost's haunting progeny.

THE SUNK COST FALLACY

A sunk cost is a cost that has already been incurred and cannot be recovered; therefore, it should not be relevant to decisions about future investments. At least, that is the theory.

---

83   Erica Goode, "A Conversation with Daniel Kahneman; On Profit, Loss and the Mysteries of the Mind," *New York Times*, November 5, 2002.
84   Daniel Kahneman, *Thinking, Fast and Slow* (New York: Farrar, Straus and Giroux, 2011), 300.

In real life, people very much care about sunk costs, as anyone can attest who has attended an event they were no longer interested in simply because they had already paid for the ticket. In the context of sales, a prospect or customer's attachment to products and services they have already paid for—their sunk cost—can motivate them to resist change simply because they feel committed after having put money into their current systems. This is known as the sunk cost fallacy.

You can manage a prospect's attachment to products and services they have already paid for by focusing attention on the way in which those systems are currently incurring losses, and how making a change would prevent those losses. Assuming there are quantifiable ways to show that the prospect's current products and services are themselves driving losses—which your product or service will remedy—simply steer attention toward those ongoing, quantifiable losses and share how you may be able to limit or prevent them.

ZERO-RISK BIAS

The second major effect of the fearful ghost of loss aversion is a tendency to prefer the elimination of a specific risk entirely—even when alternative options produce a greater overall reduction in risk. If one solution eliminates a process that created 10% of your problems, while another solution eliminates 20% of your problems overall but does not eliminate any one specific process, zero-risk bias indicates that people are likely to prefer the former, even though they should like the latter twice as much.

Although the broadly accepted rational approach begs salespeople to focus on solutions that will provide the best absolute outcome—those that will eliminate the highest number of inefficiencies—your customers are not perfectly rational, are they? The lesson for salespeople regarding the zero-risk bias is pretty straightforward: highlight the ways your product or service will be able to eliminate risks, and tread more lightly with the ways you are only able to partially mitigate risk.

Therefore, when discussing your solution, showcase those aspects that will fully eliminate specific issues— while, of course, not forgetting to highlight those aspects that will materially reduce other inefficiencies. You will find your pitch is much better received by the at-times-irrational human being sitting across from you.

REGRET AVERSION[85]

When making decisions under conditions of uncertainty, people often anticipate a feeling of regret if they make the wrong decision (refer back to my hesitance to cut the cable cord). They fear that their choice will be less than optimal, and, as with the zero-risk bias, they incorporate their desire to eliminate or reduce the possibility of that regret into their ultimate choice. This regret aversion is the final effect of the loss aversion ghost.

As a salesperson, you should expect your prospects to anticipate regret if they change from a current

---

85   For the millennials in the audience, FOMO (fear of missing out) is a derivative of regret aversion. FOMO is basically anticipation of the regret you will feel for having been left out of something, based on the fear that you may have somehow made a less-than-optimal decision that led to your exclusion.

service or product. Knowing that they will fear regret of any kind, do your best to steer those regretful feelings toward the gains that would not be realized by deciding not to decide.

Let your prospect know that you expect them to have second thoughts, that it would be abnormal if they did not—and then highlight all the good that will be realized when they make a change, specifically, good that they will continue to miss out on. Do not be shy about reiterating all the positive effects that making a change will have. Repetition of the good that will come with changing flips the regret aversion effect on its head, causing prospects to fear missing out on all the positive benefits of making a change.

As these three loss-aversion effects illustrate, the way options or ideas are framed is critically important. **Your prospects will fear loss no matter what; the question is, which losses will they be focused on?**

Although the concept of loss aversion is not without its detractors,[86] that debate is not material to this discussion. The important point here is that the decision-makers you will be selling to and working with will fall somewhere on the loss-aversion spectrum. Your job is to listen and figure out their unique sensitivity to loss. One way to do this is to coordinate loss aversion with the buyer-type chart introduced in the previous chapter.

---

86   Critics suggest that loss-aversion findings have been over-interpreted, highlighting studies that show overweighting of large losses, but little to no weighting for small losses. Some also claim that people are maximizing time averages, not expected value. Our discussion is focused on decisions centered around purchases and investments significant enough to cross the "large" threshold, thereby negating the first critique. The second is an intellectual point that is lost deep in the academic weeds of ergodicity and probability: see Jason Collins, "Kahneman and Tversky's 'Debatable' Loss Aversion Assumption," *Jason Collins Blog*, September 10, 2019, https://jasoncollins.blog/kahneman-and-tverskys-debatable-loss-aversion-assumption/.

Once you have a handle on where a prospect or customer falls on the loss aversion spectrum, you will be able to frame your value proposition in a way that best matches their unique perception of the world, mitigating the loss aversion ghost's effect on how they think about changing to your product or service. Presenting your value proposition either as a way to realize a gain or a way to prevent a loss will have a profound effect on how it is received. Choose wisely.

Before you launch into a pitch regarding the benefits of switching to your product or service, you need to have a good understanding of the sunk costs your prospect may be hesitant to abandon, those areas where you will be able to eliminate rather than minimize risk, and those areas in which your prospect is most sensitive to avoiding regret.

This can be accomplished—like so much of the guidance provided in this book—by actively listening and seeking to understand what is really important to the person you are trying to work with. Only by listening can you delicately address these critical biases and better guide their attention toward the opportunities they may already be missing out on.

Throughout your conversations with your prospects and customers, focus on developing an understanding of what losses they fear a change will bring. Then, rather than trying to assuage their fears or tell them they are meaningless, move away from their fear of change entirely and redirect their thinking by reframing the situation in terms of the losses they *should* be worried about—the losses that are already being incurred.

When working with current customers, you can use the converse process. Focus the conversation around the "optimal" aspects of working with your product or service and emphasize the relative losses that may be incurred in switching to another provider.

Unfortunately, the fear of loss can manifest in other, more subtle ways as well. Frustratingly, even if you succeed in identifying your prospect's particular sensitivity to loss and framing your pitch accordingly, you will still have to wrestle with the inertia that pulls them toward sticking with what they already know.

STATUS QUO BIAS

Albert Einstein published his theory of general relativity in 1915, illustrating that massive objects warp space-time, which we feel as gravity. More specifically, the theory refers to the relativity of motion.

Think of the theory of general relativity in terms of walking on a treadmill. The speed you are walking is relative to the speed of the treadmill's belt (the part you are walking on). Your speed relative to the room is zero, because you are effectively walking in place. And your speed relative to the sun is sixty-seven thousand miles per hour, because that is how fast the earth moves around the sun. All three of these "speeds" are accurate, depending on your perspective. That is the theory of general relativity.[87]

Understanding that something as objective as speed is impacted by relativity, you can imagine just how important relativity is to human beings' subjective experience of the real world. As far as people see the world, their lives, and the decisions they make, everything really is relative.

---

87   Another consequence of special relativity is that matter and energy are interchangeable via the famous equation $E = mc^2$ (in which E stands for energy, m for mass, and c^2 the speed of light multiplied by itself).

In terms of the sales cycle, every decision a prospect makes will be evaluated relative to the status quo.

The status quo bias, the second of our fearful ghosts, is basically behavioral science's explanation for the human tendency to prefer the current state of affairs to anything novel or unfamiliar, anything uncertain. The certainty provided by the status quo is why people prefer not making a change. If a person stays with the status quo, they know that they are likely to get the same outcome they have always gotten, and therefore are certain to avoid any new loss.

Recall the anecdote I shared with you at the very beginning of our journey: the story of my fidelity to Leopold's beef short rib. The punchline of the story was that, despite the short rib's great qualities, what kept me coming back to it was the fear that nothing else would be as good— the uncertainty of not knowing what another option would taste like. And, as we discussed before, I am not alone in this. Fear of uncertainty haunts everyone, including your prospects and customers.

In the parlance of behavioral science, the status quo is known as a *default option*. Default options are predetermined courses of action taken if the decision-maker decides to do nothing. To keep it simple, you may think of default options as "deciding not to decide" options; deciding not to decide is almost always easier than deciding to do something, because it requires little to no additional mental effort from the decision-maker.

The fact that the status quo is the default option in the minds of decision-makers is completely overlooked by many sales systems. Which is understandable, given the generally accepted rational view of the sales cycle. When the sellers and buyers involved in the sales cycle are assumed to be *Homo economicus*, there is no need to give special attention to any status quo or default, because perfectly rational people would not prefer default options to begin with. Unfortunately, *Homo economicus* we are not.

The status quo bias is one of the most powerful cogs in our mental machinery, and it is omnipresent throughout the entire sales cycle. To fully appreciate the strength and influence of the status quo bias, consider a fascinating thought experiment by Felipe De Brigard[88] (which will probably remind you more than a little of the *Matrix* trilogy).

> *It is Saturday morning and you are planning to stay in bed for at least another hour when all of a sudden you hear the doorbell. Grudgingly, you step out of bed to go open the door. On the other side there is a tall man, with a black jacket and sunglasses, who introduces himself as Mr. Smith. He claims to have vital information that concerns you directly. Mildly troubled but still curious, you let him in.*

> *"I am afraid I have some disturbing news to communicate to you," says Mr. Smith. "There has been a terrible mistake. Your brain has been plugged by error into an experience machine created by neurophysiologists. All the experiences you have had so far are nothing but the product of a computer program designed to provide you with pleasurable experiences. All the unpleasantness you may have felt during your life is just an experiential preface conducive toward a greater pleasure.*

---

88   Taken from Felipe De Brigard, "If You Like It, Does It Matter If It's Real?," *Philosophical Psychology* 23, no. 1 (February 2010): 43–57.

"Unfortunately, we just realized that we made a mistake. You were not supposed to be connected; someone else was. We apologize. That's why we'd like to give you a choice: you can either remain connected to this machine (and we'll remove the memories of this conversation taking place) or you can disconnect. However, you may want to know that your life outside is not at all like the life you have experienced so far."

What would you choose?

When De Brigard posed this question to his participants, a shocking 59% chose to stay connected to the machine. That's right. With no less than the very nature of reality at stake, a solid majority of people still demonstrated a preference for the current state of affairs, choosing the blue pill and the status quo of remaining connected to the Matrix instead of the red pill and the unknown risk of discovering what the real world had to offer.

The Force is strong with the status quo bias. Really strong. And one of the primary reasons for this is that people seek out information that validates what they already believe is true.

When making decisions under uncertain circumstances, people seek out information that will reduce their uncertainty and the fear and discomfort it brings. However, not all forms of information will reduce an individual's uncertainty, even if the information is logically related to the decision at hand. People will often remain uncertain not because they have yet to find relevant information, but because they have yet to find information that confirms what they hoped to find. This is known to behavioral science as confirmation bias, and it is our final fearful ghost.

CONFIRMATION BIAS

To have confirmation bias is to seek evidence that will confirm one's existing beliefs or theories, rather than validation of beliefs or theories that contradict your own.

We briefly teased confirmation bias in the System 1 and System 2 breakout box in the previous chapter as the primary mechanism that System 1 leverages in order to be fast and frugal. It is also a critical factor in understanding the strength of the status quo bias and the resistance salespeople experience when trying to affect change in their prospects and customers.

When your prospects are tasked with deciding whether or not to change products or services, the status quo bias and confirmation bias work hand-in-hand to provide the foundational reason for not making a change, simultaneously validating their preference for staying put by only accepting new information that is supportive of what they already think or believe.

Underestimate the status quo bias and confirmation bias one-two punch and you will find yourself knocked out of the running for your prospect's business, wondering where you went wrong. Fortunately, you are not without a means to soften this blow.

Remember the scientific method we discussed in the prospecting chapter? Not only is it a powerful tool for refining your prospecting efforts, it is also a precisely constructed antidote you may use to counter confirmation bias. In principle, the scientific method seeks to *disprove* a hypothesis or theory, which a counterpunch to confirmation bias's search for validating evidence.

Once again, this will require active listening.[89]

When communicating with your prospects, first try to understand what assumptions they are making and use the logic of the scientific method to sort out which of their objections are grounded in reason and which are reflective of a confirmation bias. Your goal is not to prove that your prospect is wrong—nobody likes to be wrong, remember?—but to judiciously challenge some of the assumptions they are making.

The best way to question your prospects' assumptions— assuming you have established a strong relationship with them already—is to have an "adult conversation" with them centered around issues where you can see their resistance. Do not shy away from asking hard questions or challenging their assumptions. If you have shown them that you are sincerely interested in helping, they will be open to a little pushback.

Up to this point, I have mentioned many times that rationally debating on the merits of your product or service will not get you very far. However, while I am arguing that rational arguments are overrated as an effective tool in the sales cycle, they obviously have their place.

Once you understand the root of a prospect's resistance, you will be better equipped to select those rational arguments that will be most effective for a particular circumstance. You will be able to use your awareness of their motivations to center your points around values you know they care about or fears that they have exhibited. This way, you will be able to give your rational arguments the best possible chance of succeeding.

---

89   It truly is impossible to overstate the importance of being a good and active listener throughout the sales cycle.

———

As salespeople, we must understand that decision-making and changing do not happen in a vacuum. The starting line—the reference point—for affecting change is the status quo of whatever systems, processes, or products are currently being used. **When making decisions, your prospects cannot help but view alternative proposals in terms relative to the products and services they are currently using, which only heightens their fear of a suboptimal outcome from a change.**

The status quo of your prospects' current products and services represents certainty. The alternative products and services that you, the enterprising salesperson, are offering represent uncertainty. When presented with a choice between certainty and uncertainty, most people, most of the time, will choose the most certain thing—which is to keep doing what they are already doing.

Although often overlooked as such, loss aversion, the status quo bias, and confirmation bias are relentless competitors; underestimate them at your peril. Instead, if you pay attention to their effects and use the suggestions above, you can begin to notice when your customers' resistance comes from the fearful ghosts.

Alas, the fearful ghosts are not the only ghouls that haunt your prospects' decision-making. We also need to be on the lookout for the busy ghosts that distract prospects and take their energy away from thinking about changing.

SQUIRREL!

*"Attention isn't free, that's why
we have to pay for it."*
—Anonymous

Once you have earned the opportunity to meet with a prospect or client, research from the RAIN Group[90] indicates that you will only be given five to ten minutes[91] to prove your value.

If you fail to grab a prospect's attention in that five to ten minutes, they will politely go through the motions for the rest of your meeting, tell you "thanks, but no thanks," and then show you the door and move on to the next thing clamoring for their attention. Such limited attention can be especially daunting for us salespeople, who, by the very nature of our jobs, are responsible for grabbing and holding another person's attention.

The simple reason your prospects barely give you the time of day is that they are already paying attention to far too much other stuff and they just cannot pay any more.

As a rule, most people—your prospects and customers included—move about their lives with their attention fractured. They are constantly bombarded by an endless variety of distractions, leaving them feeling perpetually busy and stressed out. Recall the study[92] from the previous chapter that found that human beings have an average of *6,200 thoughts per day.*

90   Mike Schultz, Bob Croston, and Mary Flaherty, *Top Performance in Sales Prospecting Benchmark Report*, RAIN Group, 2018.
91   *Of course* these time frames might be slightly longer or shorter, but the point is that your prospect's attention is limited.
92   Julie Tseng and Jorden Poppenk, "Brain meta-state transitions demarcate thoughts across task contexts exposing the mental noise of trait neuroticism," *Nature Communications* 11, no. 3480 (2020).

That we only have so much attention to give is a central tenet of behavioral science. It is one of the foundational reasons we often behave in seemingly irrational ways, as the brain has had to evolve methods to cope with the sheer volume of thoughts and stimuli we encounter on a daily basis.

Human beings do have a tremendous ability to focus our attention—sometimes. We are capable of achieving flow states[93] where we enter "the zone" and lose track of time for being so singularly focused on what we are doing. But flow states are the exception, and during the sales cycle you are unlikely to encounter somebody experiencing one.

The limited and fleeting nature of human attention is not a newly discovered concept. All the way back in ancient Sumer—humanity's first great civilization—wisdom literature informed the people that they "should pay attention."[94] However, it has only been around seventy years since a theory was developed to properly define it.

In the 1950s, American economist, political scientist, and cognitive psychologist Herbert Simon introduced his theory of *bounded rationality*, formally codifying the phenomena of limited human attention. Understanding this theory will help us see fundamentals of why the busy ghosts have so much influence on the human mind.

---

93   The mental state in which a person performing an activity is fully immersed in a feeling of energized focus, full involvement, and enjoyment in the process of the activity.

94   Jacob Klein and Nili Samet, "Religion and Ethics in Sumerian Proverb Literature," in Marbeh okmah: *Studies in the Bible and the Ancient Near East in Loving Memory of Victor Avigdor Hurowitz,* ed. S. Yona et al. (Winona Lake, IN: Eisenbrauns, 2015), 321.

BOUNDED RATIONALITY

The concept of limited attention flies in the face of rational choice theory. As we discussed in the introduction, rational choice theory argues that the rational agent takes account of all available information, including potential costs, benefits, and probabilities, in determining their preferences and acts according to what is in their best self-interest. And they are expected to do so within a moment's notice.

Given the contemporary acceptance of behavioral science and our current understanding of the ghosts in the machine, it is stating the obvious to say that human rationality does not, in fact, come instantly and without limit.

Our current understanding of humanity's limited attention began to crystalize with Simon's Models of Man, published in 1957, in which he coined the term bounded rationality. When making decisions, bounded rationality tells us that individuals are limited by three variable factors:

1. The difficulty of the decision problem
2. The limitations of the mind
3. The time available to make the decision

The main point of bounded rationality is that most people, most of the time, are only partly rational. In his words, "boundedly rational agents experience limits in formulating and solving complex problems and in processing . . . information."[95] Therefore, agents (that is, people) use heuristics (that is, mental shortcuts) to make decisions, rather than precisely optimized rules.

---

95   Herbert A. Simon, *Models of Man* (New York: Wiley, 1957).

Whenever I think about humanity's limited capacity for attention I am always reminded of dogs. The dogs in the movie *Up*, that is.

In the movie, our heroes—Carl and Russell—cross paths with a pack of dogs during their search for Paradise Falls. These dogs have been equipped with special collars that enable them to speak. As the events of the story unfold, from time to time, without warning, the dogs will interrupt whatever they happen to be doing, jerk their attention off into the distance, and shout, "Squirrel!"

Instantly the whole pack drops everything and focuses all their attention on the mere possibility that a squirrel may be loitering in the distance. This behavior reveals, in a deliciously truthful way, just how limited a dog's attention is. I find this to be the best running joke in the movie.

I laugh because, from a behavioral science perspective, these dogs are us.

Like them, our attention is limited. Like them, our attention can be ripped from one thing to the next with relative ease. And, just like those dogs, we are incapable of focusing, in an efficient and effective way, on two things at the same time.

As I mentioned earlier, people *do* have the ability to think clearly and rationally by consciously and effortfully engaging the deliberative "thinking about it" System 2 thought processes, which are less likely to be manipulated by the ghosts in the machine. However, System 2 is a limited resource, and leveraging it requires tradeoffs.

We call it "paying attention" because attention has a price. And that price is the additional time and energy used as you shift from System 1 (i.e. autopilot) to System 2 thinking (i.e. thoughtful analysis). Using energy—like most things in life—requires a tradeoff.

According to Reuven Dukas, professor of psychology and a leading researcher of the evolutionary biology of cognition at McMaster University, "limited attention is an optimal strategy that balances effective yet economical search for cryptic objects." [96] In essence, limited attention helps an animal focus when performing a challenging task—such as the search for squirrels.

However, focusing on a cognitively challenging task also reduces an animal's ability to pay attention to other stimuli in the environment—such as the presence of predators. In effect, animals—including human beings—are unable to focus on finding food and steering clear of predators at the same time; focusing their attention on one necessarily requires taking their attention away from the other.

Limited attention is a major reason that we are not the perfectly rational, utility-maximizing *Homo economicus* that classical economic theory would have us believe.

For a better understanding of how our prospects and customers think about change and why they resist it, salespeople should approach them with the knowledge that they, too, are no more than boundedly rational agents with only so much capacity to focus their attention.

Today's hyper-stimulating modern world—which practically requires business professionals to perpetually multitask—coupled with humanity's limited capacity for attention, provides fertile ground for three ghosts in the machine

---

96   Reuven Dukas, "Causes and Consequences of Limited Attention," *Brain, Behavior and Evolution* 63, no. 4 (2005): 197-210.

that reinforce our resistance to change. I give you the busy ghosts: *the focusing illusion, the Einstellung effect*, and *choice overload*.

THE FOCUSING ILLUSION

"Nothing in life is as important as you think it is while you are thinking about it."[97] So says founding father of behavioral science Daniel Kahneman when asked to describe our first busy ghost: *the focusing illusion*.

As it turns out, it is human nature to magnify the importance of whatever happens to be top of mind—to be taken with the illusion of its importance—be it a person, place, thing, or idea.

Just like bounded rationality—of which it is a direct result— the focusing illusion was understood and communicated by people in ancient times via maxims, most famously in the Persian adage "this too shall pass." In present times, any parent who has caved in to a child begging for a new toy, only to see it lightly used and forgotten only a short time afterward, instinctually understands this.

The focusing illusion affects the way prospects think about the possibility of changing. By default, they are focused on what they are currently doing, assuming that whatever got them this far will keep them going tomorrow. This creates the perspective that the products and services they are currently using, as well as the companies that provide those products and services, are critically important to their success and probably not worth switching away from—a big problem for the prospecting salesperson.

However, by diverting attention from the day-to-day

97   Kahneman, *Thinking, Fast and Slow, 402.*

mechanics of what is currently being done and focusing attention on what would be done in a more ideal scenario, you can lessen the effect of the focusing illusion, and the importance prospects place on what they are currently doing, while simultaneously getting them to focus on how they would *like* things to be, which will ideally align with your value proposition.

Of course, the focusing illusion can work in the other direction as well. For the prospect or customer who has become focused on making a change, nothing they are currently doing will seem as important as taking steps toward making said change. In many respects, this is the ultimate goal, the dream scenario for the salesperson trying to affect change.

THE EINSTELLUNG EFFECT

Ever heard the saying "to a hammer, everything is a nail"? Though it has been attributed to the likes of the Bible, Buddha, Mark Twain, and Abraham Maslow, we are not exactly sure who first uttered this quippy little phrase. Nonetheless, it perfectly encapsulates our second busy ghost: *the Einstellung effect*.

Also known as *the law of the instrument*, the Einstellung effect refers to the human predisposition to solve problems in a specific and familiar way, even though a better way may exist. Perhaps because it is easier to access in our minds and requires less mental effort, the familiar way has an ironclad grip on our attention, literally blinding us to other possibilities.

Together with the focusing illusion, the Einstellung effect makes it challenging for any of us to recognize that there might be other, equally efficient, potentially better ways to do something—even though that is almost always the case.

Like a carpenter who is just *so* comfortable with a hammer, your prospects are accustomed to and comfortable with the products and services they are currently using. They are likely to resist the idea that a change might be useful because of this attachment to the way things are already being done. However, just like that carpenter, who may use his trusty hammer simply because it is the way he is used to doing it—pounding in a bunch of nails where a few screws might work much better—your prospects likely are stretching their current vendors' products and services to uses for which they are not optimally suited.

The Einstellung effect presents an opportunity to the salesperson who can recognize the instances in which their prospects have overstretched the intended capabilities of their current vendors' products and services. These mismatches invariably create operational inefficiencies for your prospects. Those inefficiencies are precisely what salespeople need to be looking for when attempting to influence the way their prospects think about changing.

Managing the impact of the Einstellung effect is done in much the same way you manage the Focusing illusion. Get your prospects to start thinking and talking about the way they *want* things to work, which will steer their attention from the way things are currently being done, diminishing its importance.

With their focus pulled away from their current processes and systems, prospects will be more open to considering different ways of doing things, especially if there is a gap between what they are currently doing and the picture they paint of what they would like to be doing.

CHOICE OVERLOAD

Ever had the feeling of being overwhelmed with options when trying to decide what to do?[98] That is the choice overload ghost at work.

People are able to deal with a few options at a time and still make rationally optimal decisions. However, present someone with more than a few options—which salespeople and marketing folks often do, assuming more is better—and analysis paralysis quickly sets in.

Having too many choices effectively overwhelms a person's decision-making abilities, freezing them in their tracks. When that happens, people lean even harder on the ghosts in the machine for help making decisions, creating an environment that is anything but rational.

This is the emotional environment salespeople should expect when communicating with prospects who are already paying attention to too many things—as professional decision-makers almost always are.

Choice overload leads to a myriad of decision-making irrationalities, but two effects in particular are worth remembering and preparing for. If you like, you can consider these more specific effects the offspring of the busy ghost of choice overload.

PARKINSON'S LAW OF TRIVIALITY

When making decisions, members of a group or organization tend to give disproportionate weight to trivial issues. This happens because people feel the need to validate their worth during the decision-making process. In trying

---

to validate themselves, people are more likely to speak up about the aspects with which they are most comfortable and confident. This is the Parkinson's law of triviality effect.

In a group setting—which has become the norm for professional decision-making—this inevitably focuses the conversation on the elements that team members are more likely to feel confident about: the simpler, relatively less important aspects of a decision.

The Parkinson's law effect dictates that professional decision-making is penny-wise and pound-foolish. Based on time and energy spent, sweating the little things ends up being more of a priority than tackling the big, complex, and more important things.

Accordingly, you would do well to focus your messaging on two or three critical areas and do everything in your power to keep conversations with your prospects and customers focused on those issues, rather than spiraling off into trivial details. Otherwise, you may find that you spend most of the limited time you have with a prospect discussing points that are ultimately unimportant.

Unfortunately, in the vacuum in which this book is presented, it is difficult to be more specific in laying out guidance on this point. The key takeaway is that you are better off foregoing attempts to cover every area in which your solution will differ from the current practices; instead, focus your energy on those few areas that will have significant impact, thereby nudging the conversation away from more trivial issues.

DECISION FATIGUE

Anyone who has any level of experience playing sports knows the game is physically harder in the fourth quarter. It is harder to move. It is harder to breathe. It is harder to fight off your opponent. Everything is just harder. The same is true for our mental capacities when we are inundated with decisions that must be made. This is decision fatigue effect.

Decision-making exhausts the mind just like the game exhausts the body. The decision fatigue effect is that burnt-out feeling you have after taking a particularly challenging test. You are capable of making decisions after taking a brutal test, but doing so feels harder, it takes more effort, and you would really just like a break from deciding. Some decision-makers have more endurance than others, just like some athletes are in better shape than others, but eventually fatigue sets in for everyone.

If a person is forced to make decisions when they are already mentally exhausted, the "irrational" influences of the ghosts in their mental machine exert more influence on the outcome of their decisions—which is exactly what salespeople should try to avoid.

Learn to recognize the telltale signs of mental exhaustion. Is the prospect yawning? Are they easily distracted? Has their gaze lost focus?

Has their posture shifted from upright and at attention to slumped back? In other words, as we discussed in the bonus section of Relationship Building, you need to read the room.

While each person has their own unique mental exhaustion cues, these cues will be obvious to the salesperson who has been actively listening. As soon as you notice them, you are better off wrapping it up for the day, or at least taking a break, than you are trying to push through and force more decisions to be made.

To avoid choice overload and its associated decision-making irrationalities—Parkinson's law of triviality and decision fatigue—salespeople would do well to limit the number and variety of options they present to their prospects and customers. Various studies indicate that decision-making processes get jammed up once you push past six options, but in truth there is no "right" number of options. That will depend on the circumstances.

The important thing to remember is that, when trying to affect change, less is actually more—less options, less trivial talking points, less distractions.

Try as we might to leverage the effortful mechanics of System 2 thinking to help us make better decisions, we humans often end up distracted and fatigued, no closer to an optimal decision and just as likely to decide not to decide. Worse, having exhausted the bounded rationality of System 2, we become more easily manipulated into irrationality and even more vulnerable to reacting instinctually and emotionally. This is the tradeoff we, both as salespeople and as ordinary human beings, make when leveraging

System 2, and it is the fundamental challenge presented by the busy ghosts in the machine.

Collectively, the busy ghosts—the Einstellung effect, the focusing illusion, and choice overload—increase the likelihood that a decision will be made not to decide. Enabled by the brain's limited capacity for attention and the bounds on its rationality, they keep prospects and customers frozen with analysis paralysis, focused on what is already right in front of their faces, and forcing square pegs into round holes.

———

Ultimately, change is not something most people enthusiastically embrace; it runs counter to too many of the finely tuned evolutionary instincts that the human animal has been blessed (cursed?) with. In the sales cycle, professional decision-makers default to rejecting change because of two major factors:

- the inherent uncertainty of change
- their inability to focus on anything other than what they are currently doing.

These two macro dynamics fuel the fire for the fearful and busy ghosts, which represent the toughest challenge for a salesperson to overcome. They are your *real* competition.

By understanding why and how these ghosts work, you will be better able to manage their irrational effects and steer your prospects away from the status quo. While the fearful ghosts are too powerful and too deeply ingrained to be defeated, you can mitigate their interference with some adjustments to how you present your message and what you focus on during your interactions with your prospects.

With your newfound knowledge of decision-making irrationalities and a bit of attention management, you can deliver your messaging in the ways that will be most readily accepted by your customers, tipping the scales in favor of deciding *to* decide.

CHANGE THE FRAME AND PRIME THE PUMP

> *"...you're not telling them what to think as much as you are telling them what to think about..."*
> —Robert Cialdini

Trying to affect change through rational argument is the sales profession's original sin. The interference created by the fearful and busy ghosts is unavoidable and impossible to eliminate, especially with rational arguments. Instead, you must learn to recognize and understand when these specters rear their ugly heads—noticing how they uniquely affect each of your prospects and customers so that you may mitigate their impact, thereby increasing the odds that you will be able to affect change.

Fundamentally, the fearful ghosts frame everything that is not the status quo as scary and grounds for a potential loss. They frame anything short of the certainty provided by what is currently being done as something to avoid.

In order to temper these fears, you will need to show your prospects the world through a different frame.

FRAMING

Very few things in life are binary—black or white, right or wrong—in an objective sense. Most of a human life is spent in a fog of grey, without the benefit of clear, objective guidance regarding the best course of action. Whatever a person perceives of a situation will determine their experience of the situation's reality; hence the saying "perception is reality."

To perceive something is to see it in a particular way. That "particular way" is *framed* by the beliefs and experiences of the perceiver. The frame determines how the situation is interpreted, which dictates the response to whatever is on the other side of the frame.

Earlier, in the breakout box on prospect theory, we discussed making decisions based on the potential gains or losses relative to a specific situation. In the example we used, the situation of being broke and the situation of being a millionaire framed the potential gain of $100 in different ways, making the point that decisions are guided by reference points and the impact of *relative*—not absolute or objective—gains and losses.

Here, in discussing how to use framing to your benefit, we will focus on *re*framing the fear of loss that motivates decision-making.

Appreciating the power and effect of framing is critical throughout the sales cycle, but it is especially important in your attempts to affect change in the minds of your prospects. In order to mitigate resistance from the fearful ghosts, you will first need to understand and empathize with the frame of mind of the person in front of you—to put down your frame of the world and look through theirs. Only then can you do your best to reframe the situation so that the change you are offering does not sound so scary.

Learning to frame your arguments in the way that is most likely to influence your prospect to change begins in the relationship-building stage. When you get to the changing stage, it is impossible to use framing (or priming, which we will discuss below) without the understanding of your customer or prospect that you gain during the relationship-building process.

We have discussed throughout our journey that rational arguments are an ineffective method for affecting change. However, the truth is a bit more nuanced: rational arguments are ineffective until you understand where your prospect's resistance is coming from.

To choose an effective argument, you must be able to see the world through their eyes: What is important to them? What do they value, both in life and in their business? What do they fear about the process of changing? What needs do they have that their current services are not providing? Which of the fearful or busy ghosts might be affecting them the most?

Only if you have done the work of listening to an individual prospect and understanding the answers to these questions will you be able to effectively frame a rational argument around what is important to that person.

Mitigating the loss-aversion ghost and its effects is *all* about framing. Once you detect one of the loss-aversion effects, you can recognize what that specific customer most fears, then reframe your solution as a way to avoid it. This has the potential to turn the ghost on its head, turning it into a tool that will push the customer toward your solution rather than away from it.

The buyer-type chart we discussed at the end of Relationship Building is also an excellent tool to help you with framing. Think of the "What They Want" column as a proxy for where each type of individual falls on the loss-aversion spectrum. Laggards are the most loss-averse and innovators are the least. Apply the guidance of what the prospect wants in tandem with your understanding of what losses they fear, and you should find better ways to position your argument.

Here are a few more basic principles to frame your argument correctly for your specific audience.

- If you are trying to manage resistance to change coming from a sunk cost bias, you need to frame your solution as a way to stop losses that are currently being incurred.
- Get ahead of someone's regret aversion by reframing the issue to point out regrets they might have around all the benefits that would go unrealized, and therefore be lost, if no change is made.
- And, as a general rule, seeking out ways to show your prospect how you can eliminate risk altogether, not just minimize it, is your best defense against the zero-risk bias.

As for the ghosts of the status quo bias and confirmation bias, what is needed is a precise way to fetter out the difference between the objections a prospect will make that are grounded in logic and sound reasoning, and those that reflect a resistance to change.

Allow me to present *the Reversal Test*.

THE REVERSAL TEST

Introduced by Nick Bostrom and Toby Ord,[99] the Reversal Test is specifically designed to spot and eliminate status quo bias. It does so by asking about the opposite of an individual's point of view.

Let's pretend you sell a system that is faster than any other currently in use. If a prospect or customer were to claim that their systems were fast enough and the company would not see benefit from increased speed, to apply the Reversal Test, you would ask the customer if they would expect to see a negative effect from having slower systems.

If the customer does not think slower systems would have a negative effect, then you will know that their lack of interest in increased speed is legitimate. If, however, the customer does believe slower systems would have a negative impact, you will know that their lack of interest in increased speed is grounded in the status quo bias, because at that point it becomes clear that system speed actually is a factor in their business success.

Of course, the specific issue the question turns on—system speed, in our example—will change with each sales situation, but the framework of the Reversal Test is flexible enough to be applied to just about any issue that you come across. Simply ask the prospect about their opinion on the opposite, or negative version, of the effect they are resisting.

I especially like this tool because it is simple, straightforward, and easy to insert organically into a conversation.

---

99   Nick Bostrom and Toby Ord, "The Reversal Test: Eliminating Status Quo Bias in Applied Ethics," *Ethics* 116, no. 4 (2006): 656–79.

The Reversal Test is not a magic trick, but it can work magic in unlocking what is truly important to your prospects—therefore increasing the odds that you will be able to understand their frame of mind and affect a change.

Lastly, framing a change as something that will give your prospects greater control than they currently have will typically be received well. In many situations, uncertainty can be synonymous with lack of control. And, as we discussed earlier, uncertainty increases stress, making options that offer more control, and therefore less uncertainty, more attractive.

Remember the electric-shock study we referenced to open the section of this chapter on the fearful ghosts?[100] It demonstrated that when people feel as though they are in control, even when the thing they are in control of is going to be painful, they are less stressed. Frame your products and services as a means to greater control than the status quo, and you will have more success mitigating the fearful ghosts.

While the fearful ghosts frame change as scary, the busy ghosts interfere with a salesperson's ability to cut through the noise and present their value proposition. Fortunately, there is also a strategy salespeople can leverage in drawing the attention of their prospects, thereby mitigating the interference of the busy ghosts. If you have heard the phrase "to prime the pump" you are familiar with this chapter's attention-management solution.

PRIMING

To quote Robert Cialdini, renowned psychologist and author of *Pre-Suasion*: "...the factor most likely to determine

---

100   De Berker et al., "Computations of Uncertainty."

a person's choice in a situation is not the one that counsels most wisely there; it is the one that has been elevated in attention (and, thereby, in privilege) at the time of decision."[101]

An idea that is elevated in attention is a *primed* idea.

Cialdini goes on to say, "...to get a desired action it's not necessary to alter a person's beliefs or attitudes or experiences. It's not necessary to alter anything at all except what's prominent in that person's mind at the moment of a decision."[102] That is, priming is not about trying to tell others what to think, but rather hinting to them what to think *about*.

Putting Cialdini's argument in terms of the sales cycle provides the aha moment that sales is not about convincing another person through rational debate, but about focusing attention. A recent purchase I made illustrates his point.

I was recently listening to a podcast, and one of the advertisements that played in between segments of the show was for KiwiCo, a company that delivers kid-friendly science and art kits to your home. Although I had never heard of KiwiCo, before the show's next commercial break, I was online looking for the best subscription for my two-year-old daughter. Before the day was done, I was a freshly minted KiwiCo subscriber.

Looking back, I am surprised by how quickly I made the purchase, and how little conscious thought went into the decision. For me, buying something on impulse is an exception to a personal rule: I do not need most of the crap advertisements would have me buy. And when I do buy

101   Robert Cialdini, *Pre-suasion: A Revolutionary Way to Influence and Persuade* (New York: Simon & Schuster, 2016), 25.
102

something I saw in an ad, I usually spend an embarrassing amount of time researching it before pulling the trigger. For the KiwiCo subscription, I did no research at all.

Why was this time different? The answer is priming.

I am fortunate to have been exposed to a wide variety of wonderful educational experiences throughout my life. Education is something I value and recognize as important to the successes I have achieved. It is one of the main reasons I am confident in my ability to articulate the arguments I am making in this book. Nobody has to sell me on the importance of education; I already believe in it.

When the KiwiCo ad presented me with an opportunity to provide my daughter with a similarly wonderful educational experience, the idea that education is important jumped to the front of my mind, becoming "elevated in attention." With my focus tuned in to the value of education, I did not need to think about it or do research; I needed to find my wallet.

That is how priming works.

Priming is the brain readying itself to respond in a certain way, and it works as well as it does because, as we have discussed a number of times in this book, the human mind is an association machine. **In effect, to prime someone else is to focus their attention on something they already believe—such as my belief in the value of education—and associate it with whatever connection you are trying to make.**

Priming is how you cut through the noise and mitigate the influence of the busy ghosts.

There is one major difference between priming with mass

advertising and priming in a one-on-one or small-group sales meeting that is worth mentioning. Just like our prospecting numbers game, mass advertising has incredibly low conversion rates. Blasting messages out to large audiences that are *already* likely to be receptive to a given value prop—and therefore easily primed to receive it—is the only way to justify the time and effort involved in a massive advertising campaign.

Conversely, one-on-one and small-group sales meetings—the type that salespeople typically engage in—provide the opportunity to understand the specific things that each individual values. In this context, salespeople are able to tailor their messages to prime ideas that their prospects value and steer the conversation in that direction.

When you can first prime an important value in your prospect's mind, and then connect your product or service to that idea, showing how what you are offering aligns with that value, you will be in a very good position indeed to have prospects reaching for their wallets.

Priming is not a nefarious magic trick; it is a specialized tool only available to salespeople who are actively listening. The goal is not to manipulate your prospects—attempts to do so will always be transparent and waste the goodwill you have worked so hard to earn up to this point. Manipulation through clickbait-style priming hacks is the stuff of science fiction.

In reality, to be able to prime an idea in someone else's mind, you must first understand what is important to them—which can only be done by listening. Once you understand what they care most about, only then are you able to choose which of those beliefs or ideas to elevate in attention.

Throughout the sales cycle, while you are listening to understand your prospect, always be on the lookout for those beliefs or ideas they express that align with your value prop. Then, when the opportunity presents itself organically within the conversation, simply state the way your value prop aligns with the belief or idea you would like them to focus on. This is the most effective way for the sales professional to influence or persuade other people.

———

I will say it once more: sales, and affecting change, is about listening. Whether framing your message in order to maximize receptivity or priming those ideas that best align with your value prop, actively listening to your prospects and clients is your ticket to the dance. **Only by listening will you truly be able to understand what your prospects and customers want and affect the change you need to be a successful salesperson.**

Now that we have fully unmasked the fearful and busy ghosts and highlighted how the framing and priming concepts will mitigate their interference, we may turn our attention a powerful tool that effective salespeople use when applying all this theoretical rubber to the road.

If listening is the *how* that allows you to better frame and prime ideas, storytelling is the *what* that puts them into action.

TELL THEM A STORY

"No one ever made a decision because
of a number. They need a story."
—*Daniel Kahneman*

On November 27ᵗʰ, 2009, the Norwegian Broadcasting Corporation (NRK) broadcast a complete seven-hour train ride from Bergen to Oslo. The program was aired as part of the one-hundred-year anniversary of the Bergen Line.

This was not a half-baked attempt to fill dead airtime. It was an intentionally radical approach to television programming presented as an antidote to the overstimulating, fast and frequent cuts between scenes that dominate television production.

And it was a massive success. During the course of the broadcast, 1.2 million Norwegian viewers tuned in—roughly 20% of the total population of Norway.[103]

This seemingly inconsequential production experiment has since given birth to the *sakte-TV* (slow TV) movement, which has since taken root in Australia, Belgium, China, Hong Kong, the UK, Spain, France, New Zealand, and Sweden. On slow TV, an ordinary event is aired, in real time, in its entirety.

Believe it or not, well before Norway made it cool, the overstimulating TV capital of the world—the United States—had already dipped its toe into the slow TV pool. In 1966, New York City television station WPIX showed a film of a yule log burning in a fireplace without commercial interruption during the Christmas holiday season.

Back in Norway, the NRK followed the Bergen Line with slow TV productions of other marathon train and boat journeys. They also aired *minutt for minutt* (minute for minute) "episodes" of a bird feeder, someone knitting, a tidal current, salmon spawning, and reindeer migrating. All in real time and all absolutely uninterrupted.

103   Inger-Marit Knap Sæby, "'Bergensbanen minutt for minutt' ble helgens store snakkis," NRK, November 30, 2009, https://www.nrk.no/kultur/1_2-millioner-innom-_bergensbanen_-1.6888505.

On February 15th, 2013, the NRK broadcast a twelve-hour-long National Wood Night. The episode was inspired by the best-selling book by Lars Mytting, *Solid Wood: All About Chopping, Drying and Stacking Wood—and the Soul of Wood-Burning*. Once again, around a million Norwegians tuned in to the broadcast, which included no less than eight hours of a fire burning in real time. National Wood Night was so popular that the NRK followed it up with not one but two sequels: National Firewood Evening and National Firewood Morning.

Although Norwegians may take their passion for wood to the extreme, humans seem to have a primal attraction to fire that resonates for most people. Myself included.

As part of the capstone course of my business school curriculum, I participated in an Outward Bound weekend in the North Carolina wilderness. Although the experience was packed with team-building and self-reflection exercises, the fact that I successfully built and started a fire with nothing but flint and steel was easily the most rewarding part of the trip for me.

I am captivated by a good fire because I subscribe to the belief that learning to control fire was the most important innovation in human history. Building a fire is a visceral way for us to participate in an activity that human beings have been doing for just about as long as we have been roaming the planet.

Approximately two million years ago, the second-oldest ancestor on the *Homo* genus family tree—*Homo erectus*—developed the ability to control fire, providing two things that were critical in our genus's ascendance to the top of the food chain.

First, fire provides protection. It gives warmth and shelter from freezing temperatures. Its light provides visibility for us at night while simultaneously deterring nocturnal predators unaccustomed to its brightness. And its smoke repels all manner of pesky insects.

Second, fire makes food much easier to eat. Eating raw food takes a long time. Chimpanzees spend upwards of eight hours per day chewing raw food enough to make it digestible. The same was likely true of our ancestors before they learned to control fire. Cooked food can be chewed and digested in a fraction of that time. Further, more accessible nutrients meant that our ancestors were able to eat a lot more, which led to the evolutionary advantage of stronger bodies and the increased cognitive capacities and abilities from larger brains, launching us from the middle of the food chain straight to the top.

When they had light on-demand in the dark and needed less time out of each day to feed themselves, our ancestors suddenly found themselves with a lot more free time. Being especially social creatures, they naturally filled up much of this newfound free time with social interaction. This is particularly true of time spent around the protection of the fire in the darkness of night.

For the first time, instead of just huddling together, chewing food, sleeping, and waiting for morning light, these ancient people were free to spend the nighttime hours socializing and playing, reflecting on the day's events, and—most importantly—telling each other stories.

The opportunity to spend significant amounts of time around the campfire telling each other stories drove three consequential outcomes for our ancient ancestors—outcomes that remain relevant to this very day.

First, storytelling enabled the passing on and building up of knowledge. So far as we know, outside of the *Homo* genus, no other animal learns from the experiences of others in this way. Being able to accumulate and expand our knowledge with each successive generation provided our ancestors—and, eventually, us—with a tremendous evolutionary advantage. Storytelling is how we became the most intelligent apes.

Second, stories began to function as a sort of moral compass. After making the social leap, it was critical for our ancestors to communicate the moral value of cooperation, which had been of limited importance outside of immediate family members in the safety of the forests but was highly relevant to life in the open savanna. For tens of thousands of years, stories have been the primary mechanism for teaching individuals within a larger group or society how to find a balance between their selfish instincts and the need for cooperation.

Third—and most relevant to our present discussion of changing—storytelling reinforced the human instinct to find causality in life by creating links between causes and effects. The importance of causality, reinforced by its use as a basic narrative device in storytelling, makes it our most effective priming and framing tool.

CAUSALITY

As we have discussed at length, our minds operate as association machines, with the fast and frugal operations of our System 1 thinking leveraging those thoughts and ideas that are most readily available. Those available thoughts are made so via the associative links in the brain that create the thought patterns beneath the things we think and believe.

Put another way, associative links are the pathways our brains use to quickly and easily connect thoughts and ideas to whatever is top-of-mind.

David Hume, Scottish Enlightenment philosopher and economist in the 1700s, identified three principles of association.[104]

- **Resemblance**—basically, the representativeness concept we discussed in the relationship building chapter: assessing the similarity of objects or people and grouping them together around a general prototype that represents each individual within that group. New things that are sorted into this group then become connected with the associated ideas as well. This drives the lazy ghosts of stereotyping and the in-group bias that we discussed in that chapter as well.
- **Contiguity in time and place**—a fancy way of saying that things that happen near each other and/or around the same time tend to become associated in our minds.
- **Causation**—the influence by which one event—the cause—contributes to the production of another event—the effect. In other words, our minds associate two elements with each other via cause and effect, or at least perceived cause and effect.

Hume argues that causation is the strongest of the three elements of association because it establishes links between our present and past experiences and our expectations about the future, giving us the frame of reference that "all reasonings concerning matters of fact seem to be founded on the relation of cause and effect."[105]

104   "David Hume," Stanford Encyclopedia of Philosophy, April 17, 2019, https://plato.stanford.edu/entries/hume/#:~:text=Hume%20identifies%20 three%20principles%20of,because%20the%20picture%20resembles%20her.
105   David Hume, *An Inquiry concerning Human Understanding* (London: J. B. Bebbington, 1861), 17.

Although imperfect as a mental shortcut, the human tendency to believe in causality and consequences is also evolutionarily advantageous, because the consequences of ignoring a potential threat are greater than the consequences of fearing a threat that is not there. If you see what looks like the imprint of a large predator's foot in the mud, even if you are not *certain* of the cause, it is better to assume that a large predator is the cause of the imprint and remove yourself from the area to avoid getting eaten than it is to assume it is just a random imprint in the mud and continue loitering about.

Further, while huddled around the fire later that night with the rest of your tribe, wanting to share your harrowing experience with maximum effect, you would likely tell the story with an element of causality, as though you were certain that the footprint had been caused by a predator that was actively stalking you—heightening the drama and enrapturing your audience. If you did not, you would not make for a very good storyteller, and the rest of the tribe would probably let you know as much.

Telling the story like this would not only be dramatic and memorable; it would also serve as a reminder for others in your group of the link between footprints, large predators, and potential danger.

According to influence expert Robert Cialdini, presumed causality, especially when acquired through channeled attention, is also a big deal for creating influence. In other words, whether the cause-and-effect link has been factually verified or not, the description of a causality relationship primes another person's limited attention.

Causality—and its use in storytelling—resonates in the mind of the human animal. It sticks.[106]

What does *not* stick in the mind of the human animal is statistics. Statistics do not provide a sense of causation, leaving them unassociated in our minds. Without linked associations, our frugal System 1 does not know what to do with these miscellaneous data points, making them ineffective as change agents.

In their 2007 book *Made to Stick*, brothers Chip and Dan Heath discuss some eye-opening research that Chip did with his students at Stanford University. The students were given data on crime patterns in the US and told to give a one-minute presentation to their class. On average, the students used 2.5 statistics in their presentations; only one in ten students framed their presentation as a story.

Approximately ten minutes after the presentations ended, the students were asked what they remembered of the presentations they had just witnessed. Amazingly, only 5% of the students remembered the statistics, while 63% recalled the stories that had been shared. Let me put that another way: nineteen out of twenty students could not remember the data they had *just* heard, but twelve out of twenty remembered the stories.[107]

In the behavioral science community, the stickiness of stories and our Teflon-like response to statistics is represented by the *identifiable victim effect*.

---

106   There is a reason I have incorporated so many personal anecdotes and human-interest stories throughout this book. You are much more likely to remember them than you are the (arguably more important) facts and figures I have shared.
107   Chip Heath and Dan Heath, *Made to Stick: Why Some Ideas Survive and Others Die* (New York: Random House, 2007), 242-43.

IDENTIFIABLE VICTIM EFFECT

The identifiable victim effect is the tendency for individuals to offer greater aid when a specific, identifiable person—the victim—is in need, and less aid when an anonymous group has the same exact need. According to Thomas Schelling, the American economist credited with conceptualizing this effect, seeing the plight of a specific individual invokes, "anxiety and sentiment, guilt and awe, responsibility and religion...[but] most of this awesomeness disappears when we deal with statistical death."[108]

Identifiable victims are just that—identifiable. We know their story, their background, their family, their hopes and dreams, and our capabilities for empathy and sympathy tend to get to work. On the other hand, anonymous groups are just that, anonymous. They have no story, no background, no family, hopes, or dreams. Identifiable victims are vividly represented in our minds. Anonymous ones are dull and abstract.

In addition to delivering causality—which our brains feed on—having an identifiable victim is one of the major reasons that stories are more memorable and more moving than standalone statistics.

Identifiable victims elicit emotion where unassociated information does not.

Research[109] demonstrates that emotion has a strong influence on a variety of our cognitive processes, including attention and memory. Emotion focuses attention and

---

108   T. C. Schelling, "The Life You Save May Be Your Own," in *Problems in Public Expenditure Analysis*, ed. S. B. Chase, Jr., (Washington, DC: Brookings Institution, 1968).

109   Chai M. Tyng et al., "The Influences of Emotion on Learning and Memory," *Frontiers in Psychology* 8, no. 1454 (2017).

facilitates the encoding of memory. Emotion also assists in the retrieval of information, paving a path of less resistance for memories tied to emotions to surface. The connection between emotion, attention, and memory explains the Heath brothers' findings about the students' presentations and goes a long way toward explaining why stories are more effective than statistics as tools for affecting change.

For our purposes in discussing changing, the stories salespeople tell need to have an "identifiable victim" that will provoke feelings in their prospects—and they need to steer clear of statistics that represent an anonymous group in which awesomeness goes to die.

THE FORMULA

Too often, throughout the sales cycle, salespeople focus their messaging on data and statistics that favor their product or service, under the rational assumption that the product with the best data and statistics will win the day. However, as we have discussed ad nauseam, people are not rational. Without a story connecting them to the product—without causality and emotion—the random facts or data that salespeople present are unmoving and easily forgotten.

Statistical and factual insights can be communicated much better when they are dressed up with a causal story. If this sounds intimidating, do not worry—you do not have to recreate the wheel here. Courtesy of the storytelling geniuses at Pixar, there is a tried-and-true formula that salespeople can use to better frame and prime their rational talking points.

The Pixar formula, which you can recognize in each of their wildly successful movies, goes as follows.[110]

Once upon a time there was ....
[a character, or, in this case, a customer from a success story]

Every day, ...
[the same old thing happened, that is, the customer continued with
their status quo systems, which had some problems]

One day, ...
[something changed, that is, the customer switched to
your product or service]

Because of that, ...
[the effects of this change; in the case of sales,
they should probably be positive]

Because of that, ...
[the (positive) effects of the previous step; and so on, if necessary]

Until finally, ...
[a happy ending]

In the context of this chapter's focus on changing, it helps to think of step one, "Every day..." as representing the status quo, while step two, "One day..." represents making a change. Your prospect is currently living the "every day." Your goal is to get them to take the leap into "one day..."

This formula is particularly useful in sharing customer success stories. Allow me to demonstrate with an amalgamation of success stories I personally experienced during my time selling newswire distribution. I have slightly modified

---

110   Emma Coats (@lawnrocket), "#4: Once upon a time there was ___. Every day, ___. One day ___. Because of that, ___. Because of that, ___. Until finally ___. #storybasics," Twitter, May 11, 2012, 2:37 p.m., https://twitter.com/lawnrocket/status/201018115604230146

the Pixar formula to remove the fairytale dressing and better fit my story; I encourage you to do the same.

1. There was an entrepreneur who used the most popular newswire service to distribute press releases about his products.

2. Each time he sent a press release, he was upset with the cost of distribution, disappointed with the lack of response to his message, and frustrated with his lack of control in the process. He continued working with his current provider because he was unaware that there were viable alternatives.

3. After ignoring my calls for some time, he finally accepted a meeting with me. Once I had a solid understanding of his current situation, I shared with him the ways our newswire service might be able to help him out, specifically through cost reduction and increased control of the process via greater customization. After our meeting, he decided to use our service for his next few press releases.

4. Because of that, he immediately realized around a 30% reduction on the cost of distribution.

5. Because of the switch, thanks to our greater variety of targeted specialty distribution options, his press releases were better targeted and generated a significant uptick in responses.

6. Eventually, he moved all his press release distribution to our newswire service and wrote a glowing testimonial about his experience with us.

Do not make the mistake of dismissing this formula as a children's fairytale gimmick. Though it might seem simple and obvious, this is how stories are told.

Stories are driven by causation, focused on a specific identifiable person or thing. They express emotions and are framed around an understanding of the audience's wants and needs. And they enable you to dress up those otherwise unassociated data points in a package that people will remember.

Of course, there are other storytelling methods and formulas that may also work for eliciting emotion from your audience. I am a fan of the Pixar formula, but if you have another storytelling method that you find effective, use it. The takeaway here is that if you tell stories focused around the concepts we have discussed—rather than rattling off forgettable statistics—they are much more likely to resonate with your customers.

In addition, recognize that the hero of the story should always be the customer—not the salesperson or the product or service they are selling. Remember, you are just a character in their movie; they are the star.

One last storytelling tip: salience is critical to telling a truly memorable story. The more vivid, novel, and surprising the story, the more likely it is to resonate with your audience, whether it be friends and family huddled around a fire at night or a professional decision-maker consumed and distracted by the noise of modern life. Do not jump the shark[111] and excessively exaggerate your stories; rather, strive to deliver them in unexpected ways or with unexpected insights so that they really stick out.

BONUS: BLOT

There is a classic three-part presentation structure that will be familiar to anyone who has had the occasion to deliver

---

111   This is a reference to *Happy Days*—more specifically the Fonz—that seriously dates me...but it's too good not to take advantage of!

a message in front of an audience more than a few times: tell them what you are going to say; say it; then tell them what you just said. This structure is known as an Aristotelian Triptych.

Aristotle, the father of rhetoric, taught his students using this three-paneled approach—aka triptych—believing it to be the most effective means of presenting to an audience. If and when you ever need to prepare a presentation for an audience, I encourage you to do the same.

That said, I would like to focus your attention on just the first part of this triptych: "Tell them what you are going to say."

This little nugget of effective communication wisdom is often overlooked in the world of business communication. In particular, it is lost when communicating with prospects and customers via email. While I encourage you to actually speak with prospects over the phone as your primary means of communication, much of the interaction you will have with prospects and customers will be done via email; such is the nature of modern professional life.

That being the case, you need to structure your messages in ways that will maximize their effectiveness in communicating information. One of those ways—and a severely underutilized one—is to *put the bottom line on top*.

By telling the recipient what you are going to say right out of the gate, you increase the likelihood that your message will be clearly received and responded to.

In general, people are not so good at highlighting the ultimate point they are trying to make, either burying it in the middle of their message or saving it for the end like some kind of punchline. This usually results in a lack of clarity as to what you are telling or asking of your audience.

To put the bottom line on top—BLOT, for those keeping score at home—is to embrace the first step in Aristotle's triptych. If it was good enough for the father of rhetoric, it is certainly good enough for emails to your prospects.

———

Changing minds is hard. Not because decision-making is necessarily hard, although it is, but because changing from a previous decision requires that we think about the change—and, as we have seen in this chapter, thinking *itself* is hard. The times we humans struggle the most in life—especially in fending off the fearful and busy ghosts in the machine—are the times we actually have to think deeply about something.

Leveraging insights from behavioral science, we can unmask the primary ghosts that motivate our prospects and customers to resist our selling efforts and, all too often, convince them to decide not to decide. These ghosts frighten and distract decision-makers into sticking with what they already know, convincing them that changing would be riskier, keeping them intently focused on their current practices, and associating the status quo with stability and the salesperson with uncertainty and risk.

Critically, change does not come through rationality, debate, or some unspecified act of "selling." Rather, selling begins with affecting change: getting prospects or customers to the point where they are open to trying something new.

The ability to affect change first and foremost comes from understanding how people actually think about changing. Viewing change through a behavioral science lens, we can understand that our prospects are petrified of the uncertainty they confront in making decisions and have only so much capacity to pay attention, both of which offer plenty of motivation for them to stick with the status quo.

Knowing this, and engaging accordingly, you will be better able to frame your value prop in a way that is likely to be well received. When you are listening actively, you can begin to notice which fears and distractions haunt each of your prospects, then connect your product or service to the values that your customers most care about through priming—ultimately framing your solution as a way to alleviate their fears.

The tools outlined in this chapter are, once again, not a cure-all. Rather, these are easily adaptable strategies that, if used in the spirit in which they are intended, will help mitigate the fearful and busy ghosts, thereby increasing the odds that you will be able to move your prospect away from their status quo and tip the scales in favor of deciding to decide.

Even if you follow each piece of advice provided herein to the letter, you still might find yourself beating your head against the status quo wall. If that happens—and if you think that the prospect is still worth your time—go back and keep framing and priming. Eventually you will get your shot. Honestly, that's life, and anyone telling you differently is lying.

On the other hand, what if everything goes according to plan, and your prospect has asked you to propose on an upcoming purchase decision? Now what? What can you do to increase the odds that you will actually win the deal?

Good question. It is time to talk about negotiating—the other half of "selling."

NEGOTIATING

One of the luxuries of being tucked away in the ivory tower of business school, safe from the struggles of everyday life in the "real world," is the opportunity to pursue the elective study of various business-related topics. During my two-year sojourn from reality, one of my favorite just-for-fun classes was Negotiations. As an extrovert, I enjoyed the interactive nature of the subject matter. And as a behavioral science nerd, I loved learning about the theoretical underpinnings and motivations of human beings in the specific context of the negotiation setting.

Like many business-school classes, my negotiations class was largely built around and delivered via case studies. If you are unfamiliar, a case study simply outlines some business situation, real or imagined, that poses a question to which there is no clear-cut right or wrong answer. (Think of them as a cousin to role playing, which you have probably suffered through at some point in your sales career.) The idea is that more learning happens through the exchange and robust debate of ideas amongst peers than would happen with a traditional lecture, where the "right" answer is spoon-fed to you by an all-knowing professor.

While we dissected a variety of cases over the course of the semester, one in particular has always stood out in my mind. Although it is of the imagined variety, this case study beautifully illustrates how and why so many negotiations fall short of an optimal solution, due in large part to the misconceptions most people have about what it means to negotiate.

This case is about a tree.[112] More specifically, it is about the medicinal properties of a certain type of tree, and two parties with a competing interest in said tree. For purposes of simplicity, assume that this is the only type of tree in existence that can provide what each party is looking for and there is no realistic or timely way to recreate the medicinal properties of these trees.

When the case study is executed in the classroom or training setting, in order to generate the tension required to realistically execute the negotiation, each participant is only presented with the perspective, motivations, and intentions of one of the two parties. For now, I am going to assign you the role of tree owner.

You have invested significant time, energy, and money into the development of these trees, which have been genetically engineered such that you are able to extract a compound from their roots that will assist in the treatment of

112   This is based strictly on my memory of the case, as I did not save my notes from the class, nor was I able to find the case online. Although I am paraphrasing, and I'm sure I have fudged (if not completely altered) the details, the takeaways from the case should nonetheless hold.

an otherwise untreatable form of cancer. There is no alternative treatment for this type of cancer, a cancer that you are predisposed to developing.

You are wrapping up Phase I trials of your treatment, but, unfortunately, you went significantly overbudget in the process of getting to this stage of development and you do not have enough money to make it to Phase II trials. You have discussed the situation with your current investment group and they are unwilling to put any more money into what remains a fundamentally speculative endeavor. To raise the stakes, assume that you do not have the time or resources to raise funds beyond your current investor group.

As luck would have it, you are approached by another party—the non-owning party—who asks for a meeting to discuss their interest in the trees. Although you are hesitant to accept the meeting, given your investment in the trees to date and your personal motivations to cure this particular form of cancer, you accept the meeting request. Perhaps this meeting will generate the alternative source of income you need to see the project through completion (Phase IV trials and finished product distribution).

In the meeting, you learn that the non-owning party would like to buy the rights to the trees from you. They express their belief that compounds from the tree will be able to prevent a rare form of heart disease, which they have been studying for some time. They are willing to pay a premium that would represent a reasonable return for your time, effort, and expenses to date. However, in exchange, they require full ownership and control of the trees, threatening your ability to move forward with your research.

What do you do?

Take a few minutes right now to think through the possible ways this negotiation might unfold.

Is there any amount of money that would incentivize you to walk away from these trees? If so, how much? If not, why not? What will happen if you do not find another source of funding? Is there any way to work with the other party and find a win-win solution?

SELLING: PART TWO

In the previous chapter, we established that what many consider "selling" is in fact two separate components: the act of a prospect changing their mind, and the act of negotiating.

If changing is the more subtle, workmanlike half of selling, then negotiating is the more visible and glamorous half. If these two played basketball together, changing would do all the dirty work of rebounding and playing defense, while negotiating would score all the points and get all the credit for the team's success.

Do not be prematurely seduced by the draw of negotiating and rush your prospects through the changing process. Everyone changes at their own pace, and you are better off allowing them to do so. If you try to rush through changing, one of two things will happen:

- you will not be given the opportunity to negotiate, or
- your negotiation will necessarily be limited by your prospect's remaining reservations about changing.

All that said, we have now passed into the next stage in our journey. If and when you do find yourself seated at the negotiating table, your prospect and soon-to-be customer has already changed their mind and decided that they would like to start working with you. Congrats!

Up to this point in the sales cycle, you have done the heavy lifting of finding the right prospects, building a relationship with them, and mitigating their resistance to change. Now it is time to negotiate the finer points of your future working relationship.

As we have seen in our journey thus far, the ghosts in the machine create interference that often results in less-than-optimal outcomes for both salespeople *and* their prospects, and the negotiating process is no exception. During this stage, the ghosts amplify our competitive instincts and our stubborn refusal to cede ground from our stated positions. These ghosts promote irrational behaviors and perceptions that lead to suboptimal outcomes— outcomes where the best options might not even end up on the table.

Later on in this chapter, we will reveal the buying party's interests and motivations from the case of the medicinal tree and pull the curtain back on a negotiation path that most people never consider. Right now, the important thing is to know that in many negotiating situations, better outcomes are hiding just beneath the surface—only a key question or two from being uncovered.

The ghosts in the machine can, and often do, gum up the works and turn negotiating into a lose-lose situation. But by leveraging insights from behavioral science, salespeople can learn to disarm these ghosts and uncover more optimal paths. And the first step to finding more optimal paths is knowing the game you are really playing.

NEGOTIATING IS NOT ALWAYS A WIN-LOSE COMPETITION

"Only strength can cooperate."
—Dwight D. Eisenhower

"Fine. Then we'll just walk away."

This is the last thing bankers want to hear from the owners of a business in trouble.

I have spent the last ten years of my professional life as a finance professional and banker. One of the most interesting things I have learned about the relationship between banks and companies when times get tough is how much that dynamic can feel like a high-stakes game of chicken.

For those unfamiliar with the concept, the classic game of chicken is two cars racing toward a cliff to see who will go furthest before they hit the brakes to save themselves. When a company experiences challenging times, the game of financial chicken is on, and it hinges on the terms in the credit agreement[113] between the bank and the company. That credit agreement functions as a mechanism to bring both the company and bank back to the negotiating table in order to work out a new plan to help the company right the ship. This renegotiation is where the game of financial chicken typically unfolds.

During a renegotiation prompted by the company defaulting on one or more of their financial covenants, companies will generally push to see how far they can stretch the limits of what the bank is willing to accept. Conversely, the bank

---

113   The credit agreement is simply the legal document outlining the terms to which both parties have agreed pertaining to the lending/borrowing of money, including the specific steps that may be taken when certain performance metrics are not met by the company or the bank.

will generally push to impose a new set of more restrictive terms to better protect themselves.

At this point, each party can see the cliff they are racing toward; both parties are aware of the stakes if they push too far. If they cannot agree on a path forward,[114] the company is at risk of losing their business, and the bank is at risk of losing the money they have lent.

It is important to keep in mind that these types of renegotiations happen with both parties under duress. Difficult circumstances amplify the effects of the ghosts in the machine and raise the negotiation stakes, providing a fantastic laboratory for gaining insight into what does and what does not work in negotiating for optimal solutions.

One particular renegotiation I was recently involved in highlights many of the behavioral negotiating principles we will be discussing in this chapter.

Prior to this renegotiation, the bank and the company's management team had enjoyed an exceptionally strong relationship. Management had always been proactive and forthright in reporting back to the bank, above and beyond what was required of them. In turn, the bank had been very accommodating of the company's various requests for adjustments and amendments to the terms of the credit agreement, even going so far as to allow for a number of credit exceptions that were outside the terms of the credit agreement.

Approximately three years into working together, the company informed the bank that they were anticipating a significant loss and would be in default of their credit

---

114   There are alternative solutions—such as takeout by another financial institution—that I am not highlighting for purposes of illustrating my point as simply as possible.

agreement. In short, due to circumstances outside of management's control and largely driven by an industry-wide downturn, the company estimated that they would need an additional two million dollars in order to fund themselves over the next six months and get back in line with the terms of the credit agreement.

Complicating matters, the company had recently been purchased by a private equity firm,[115] representatives from which would now be taking management's place in discussions with the bank pertaining to the credit agreement. Unfortunately, the people from the bank and the private equity firm had little to no working relationship when they sat down at the negotiation table to discuss a solution to the situation.

Not long after exchanging pleasantries, the managing director[116] of the private equity firm set a decidedly combative tone to the negotiation, arguing that this was a short-term and unavoidable issue that the private equity firm and company were not responsible for, one that the bank should step up to fix with an additional extension of credit. Attempting to wrestle back control of the negotiation, the bank's portfolio manager[117] responded in kind, telling the managing director that this was, in fact, an equity issue that needed to be solved by the private equity firm, one the bank was unwilling to fix with debt.

Unfortunately, and perhaps not surprisingly, the negotiation never got past these two incompatible positions.

The combative tone set at the top of the negotiation was too much to overcome, and both sides immediately got

115   A private equity firm is simply an owner or investor in a collection of businesses, run by a management team on behalf of a group of investors.
116   Leader of the relationship team for the private equity firm
117   Leader of the relationship team for the bank

188

entrenched in defending their positions. The duration of the call was spent doing laps around the same bush: the private equity firm taking no responsibility for the current situation and throwing the bank under the bus for being inflexible; the bank holding fast to the equity versus debt argument and trying to explain that fixing the situation was the private equity firm's responsibility.

After about an hour of this song and dance, the private equity firm threatened to walk away from the business and just eat the loss if the bank would not change its position, which pretty much ended the conversation. The negotiation had reached an impasse, with each side unwilling to relent and give the other the satisfaction of winning—and both parties walked away without a way to avoid launching themselves over the cliff.

This disheartening anecdote serves to showcase one of the primary assumptions most negotiators, and probably most people, have going into this kind of interaction.

Whether haggling with a used car salesman, considering the value of medicinal trees, or debating the finer points of a credit agreement, most of the time, people assume that negotiating is a win-lose proposition. Either you maximize your outcome and minimize your opponent's, thereby "winning," or they are the ones doing the maximizing, and you are therefore "losing." Simply put, people assume negotiating to be synonymous with competing.

Much of the time, negotiating *is* a win-lose competition. But it does not always have to be.

Life is competitive. More specifically, life is naturally competitive when striving "...for a common goal which cannot be shared; where one's gain is the other's loss."[118] Common goals that cannot be shared occur whenever two or more entities—plants, animals, people, companies, etc.—vie for scarce resources—sunlight, mates, natural resources, customers, etc. Scarcity animates the loss-aversion ghost we discussed in the previous chapter, which encourages us to compete for fear of missing out.

As you will recall from our discussion of the fearful ghosts, we fear loss more than we hope for equivalent gain, and that is a big part of what drives our instinctual competitive response. In this case, what we fear is loss of relative advantage—that someone else gaining a scarce resource will necessarily mean our loss. Ultimately, this fear distills down to a fear for survival born in the fire of millions of years of evolutionary struggle. As such, it makes perfect sense that negotiating would be viewed as a competitive endeavor.

However, life is also cooperative.

As we discussed in the introduction, Dunbar's social brain hypothesis proposes that human intelligence evolved as a means of helping us survive and reproduce in large and complex social groups. Coupling this theory with the updated savanna hypothesis—that tectonic activity millions of years ago gradually replaced our ancestors' rainforest home with open savanna—von Hippel argues that our ancestors were incentivized to take a "social leap," in which natural selection began prioritizing cooperation at least as much as it did competition.

It is not a stretch to say that the incentive to share and cooperate with each other has underwritten every

---

118   Ken G. Smith, Walter J. Ferrier, and Hermann Ndofor, "Competitive Dynamics Research: Critique and Future Directions," in *The Blackwell Handbook of Strategic Management*, ed. Michael A. Hitt, R. Edward Freeman, and Jeffrey S. Harrison (London: Blackwell, 2005), 309–54.

advancement we humans have made as a species—from harnessing control of fire to exploring space. Without cooperation, nothing beyond the life our ancestors knew prior to being forced from the forest could ever have happened.

Even though competition is often considered to be the opposite of cooperation, in practical terms, mixtures of cooperation and competition are the norm throughout human society. The fact is, evolution has shaped human beings with instincts both to work together and to compete against each other; both of these forces are at work within us every day. Negotiations are no exception.

Unfortunately, the opportunity to utilize our collaborative instincts in the negotiation setting frequently goes unrecognized, especially in the business context.

Competition is a major tenet of market economies and businesses, and rightly so. We most often associate business with competition for the simple fact that companies are usually competing with at least one other firm over the same group of customers, and there are only so many of those customers to go around. Either you "win" a customer's business, or you "lose" it to your competitor.

Accordingly, negotiating in a business setting is typically framed as a win-lose situation. As a simple example salespeople will be familiar with, either the seller wins by selling something for a higher price, or the customer wins by buying something for a lower price.

However, purely focusing on competition and ignoring the wide variety of opportunities business presents for collaboration reflects a misunderstanding of the game that we are all playing.

In his most recent book—*The Infinite Game*—prolific business author and speaker Simon Sinek discusses the two types of games one can play: finite and infinite games.[119]

- *Finite games*—like basketball, or traditional video games like Mario Brothers—have players that are known and rules that are fixed, and there is an agreed-upon objective that ends the game with a winner being declared.

- *Infinite games*—like politics, or massively multiplayer online games such as World of Warcraft—can be played by players both known to us and unfamiliar, without fixed rules, and with no clear end point. In infinite games, there is no "winning" in the traditional sense. Rather, the objective of the infinite game is simply to keep playing the game.

Leaders who embrace an infinite-game mindset, says Sinek, will eventually build stronger, more innovative, and more inspiring organizations with the resilience to thrive in an ever-changing world. Likewise, approaching negotiating as an infinite game enables greater willingness to seek out creative and collaborative solutions that will invariably lead to better outcomes.

Business more closely resembles an infinite game than it does a finite one. In business there are known and unfamiliar players, there is no fixed set of rules,[120] and there is no clear end point. Yet most of your prospects and customers—and your sales competitors—are still playing the

---

119   Sinek's work builds on ideas developed by James P. Carse, who originally made the distinction between finite and infinite games. Simon Sinek, *The Infinite Game* (New York: Portfolio / Penguin, 2019).

120   *Of course* there are rules and regulations that determine what is legal and what is not, but within the confines of legality, there is no clear set of rules that govern business, as there is in more finite games like sports, etc.

wrong game. They probably see business, negotiating, and perhaps even life itself as a finite game offering a win-lose proposition, and they will respond to you accordingly.

For this, we can place the blame on the competitive ghost.

TO COMPETE OR NOT TO COMPETE

"...by integration we find a way by which both sides may get what they wish."
—Mary Parker Follett

Most people, most of the time, perceive life as a pie: fixed in size and able to be shared among only so many people. This holds true in relatively trivial and straightforward situations—like haggling over the price of a used car—as well as in complex situations that impact everyone on the planet. Take one of the most common arguments regarding the broader economy, for example.

The debate pitting the 1% against the 99%—which blames those at the top for hoarding too much and leaving too little for everyone else—is usually framed around a fixed-pie assumption. Discussions about the haves and the have-nots make the implicit assumption that only so many can "have" while the rest must, therefore, "have not." After all, there is only so much stuff to be had, right? Further, the idea of redistribution from those at the top to those at the bottom, whatever the mechanism, assumes that you must take from the haves in order to give to the have-nots, that there is no other or better way to lift up those at the bottom of the pyramid.

The point here is not to argue the merit of either side of this debate, but rather to recognize the fixed-pie assumption upon which these arguments are based and acknowledge it as a general view of the world that many people ascribe to, consciously or not, your prospects included.

In behavioral science, the fixed-pie perception is known as the *zero-sum bias*.

Joanna Rozycka-Tran of the University of Gdansk Institute of Psychology, along with colleagues, describes zero-sum thinking as "a belief system about the antagonistic nature of social relations—that one person's gain is possible only at the expense of other persons."[121] This is our competitive ghost, and when it comes to negotiations, it is a powerful force in the human mind.

ZERO-SUM BIAS

When it comes to our competitive instincts, the zero-sum bias rules over all the other ghosts in the machine.

Fortunately, understanding this ghost requires no more than a straightforward understanding of the environmental pressures that faced our ancient ancestors, with the limited availability of resources providing the key insight. The zero-sum bias was likely an evolutionary adaptation that motivated individuals and groups to compete with one another in times when resources like food, shelter, and mates were perpetually scarce. Simple.

As is the case for all the ghosts in the machine, our zero-sum bias persists despite changes in the world around us that should have motivated new and different mental shortcuts by now. As we discussed in the introduction, our internalized biases, which have served us so well for so

121 Joanna Różycka-Tran, Paweł Boski, Bogdan Wojciszke, "Belief in a Zero-Sum Game as a Social Axiom: A 37-Nation Study," *Journal of Cross-Cultural Psychology* 46, no. 4 (May 2015): 525.

long, are slow to update when the external environment changes over a relatively short period of time—even if relatively short, in this case, means tens of thousands of years.[122]

Case in point: as recently as 2015, Rozycka-Tran and her colleagues found confirming evidence in a thirty-seven-nation study[123] that people who believe that life is a zero-sum game do, in fact, engage in win-lose exchanges over limited resources. Specifically, they found that people from countries with lower gross domestic product[124] (GDP) and individuals with a lower socioeconomic status—those people who experience a life in which resources are more scarce—showed stronger-than-average zero-sum beliefs.

The zero-sum bias ghost demands that we see social interaction as competition for scarce resources, games as finite, and negotiations as winner-take-all affairs. This was evolutionarily beneficial to our ancestors. And, at first glance, it might seem natural for us to simply try to maximize our profit while taking profit away from others during negotiations.

However, the winner-take-all approach hides certain pitfalls.

The most important of these is that, if both parties assume that creating an optimal outcome for themselves requires taking something away from the other—that is, if both parties are playing the negotiation as a finite game—the opportunity to embrace more creative solutions will be ignored, and animosity will take the place of trust. A whole

---

122   Compared to the time it took our brains to evolve, relatively short is an accurate assessment of recorded history.
123   Różycka-Tran, Boski, Wojciszke, "Belief in a Zero-Sum Game," 525–48.
124   Gross domestic product is a measure of the market value of all the final goods and services produced in a country in a specific time period.

world of possibilities will be closed to salespeople before they even get to the negotiating table.

Learning to see negotiating as an infinite game—where the goal is not to "win"—is the first step toward taking the zero-sum bias's competitive blinders off and opening yourself to the possibility of letting your collaborative instincts take over. And if you are willing to take that leap of faith, it will help you to recognize the two main negotiating archetypes.

DISTRIBUTIVE VERSUS INTEGRATIVE NEGOTIATIONS

Negotiation—like many things in life—happens on a spectrum. At one end of the spectrum are winner-take-all situations. At the other end are "everybody wins" situations.

Most of the time, a negotiation will fall somewhere in between the extreme ends of this spectrum, landing closer to one end or the other. That said, you must understand the differences between these two extremes if you are to find an optimal tactical approach to any given negotiation.

Winner-take-all negotiations are distributive. In a distributive negotiation, the size of the pie—whatever is being negotiated over—is fixed and cannot be expanded or shared. Further, the pie is typically a single issue or an item that all parties are focused on. Therefore, the purpose of the negotiation is to split up (i.e., distribute) the pie amongst the negotiating parties.

(cont.)

Distributive negotiations
are characterized by relationships that are:

Short term—buyer and seller are not incentivized to work with each other in the future

Power based—tension is driven by the leverage one or more parties have over the other(s)

Transactional—the item being negotiated is standalone and one-time in nature

"Everyone wins" negotiations are integrative. In an integrative negotiation, the pie has the potential to be expanded—benefiting all parties—or shared among multiple parties, also benefiting all. In addition, there are typically multiple items being negotiated in an integrative negotiation, providing more incentive to generate creative solutions and find alternative ways to expand the pie based on the wants and needs of each party.

(cont.)

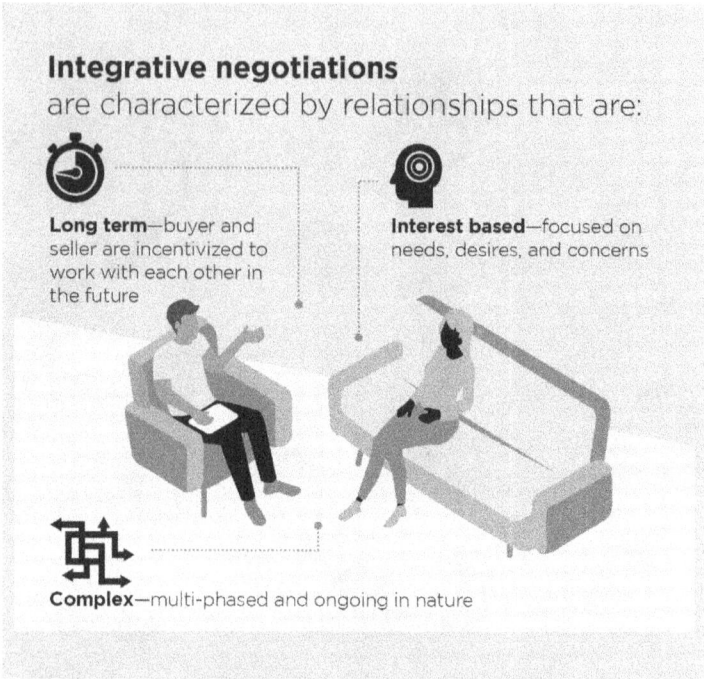

Integrative negotiations
are characterized by relationships that are:

Long term—buyer and seller are incentivized to work with each other in the future

Interest based—focused on needs, desires, and concerns

Complex—multi-phased and ongoing in nature

For every negotiation you enter into, it is going to help you immensely to figure out where the negotiation falls on the spectrum of distributive to integrative. Do not assume that every negotiation is necessarily of the winner-take-all distributive variety. Further, appreciate that there are likely to be some individual decision points within the same negotiation that are more distributive, while others might be more integrative.

Again, business, sales, and negotiating more closely resemble infinite games than they do finite ones, with known and unfamiliar players, no fixed set of rules, and no clear end points. **As such, you will find more success negotiating if you look for ways to align your interests with your prospects' and seek out integrative solutions whenever possible.**

Business, sales, and negotiating are not just about winning. Winning is important, and success is something to strive for, but being singularly focused on winning—especially when negotiating—will, ironically, lead to suboptimal solutions.

If you are skeptical about this notion, consider this: for the type of sales on which we are focused—outside, B2B, complex, recurring sales to C-level executives—your negotiations will not be a one-time affair. If you are doing your job and finding success, you will find yourself sitting across from the same decision-makers multiple times. Even though some of those negotiations will be distributive and some will be integrative, the singular outcome of one set of negotiations is not the only outcome that matters. In the long run, it is important that these customers continue to be interested in working and negotiating with you.

Staying in the game for the long haul will ultimately benefit you and your company more than one large short-term win that sours your relationship or makes a customer feel as though they have "lost." That is, if you can remember that you are playing an infinite game that requires an integrative approach, you will have more long-term success.

That said, once a negotiation is underway, there is something else good negotiators are keenly aware of. Something that may artificially limit the outcome for each party involved. Something that should demand your attention if you want to take your negotiation skills to the next level.

That something is the lifeblood of our next negotiation apparition: the stubborn ghost.

DROPPING ANCHORS

"To reach a port, we must sail—
sail, not tie at anchor"
—Franklin D. Roosevelt

Think back to the last time you were in a situation where you needed to determine the value of something you were unfamiliar with—something that had no clearly established price.

Perhaps you were thinking about buying a car that was for sale online for "best offer." Or maybe you were looking to buy some random stuff that had no price tag at a flea market or garage sale. In any case, whatever you did, I am guessing that you came up with some sort of objective measure to determine the price. I am also going to guess that you would argue that it is unlikely that arbitrary and unrelated factors otherwise influenced you, right?

Are you sure?

Dan Ariely, author of *Predictably Irrational*, investigated this question in an experiment he conducted with his graduate students at MIT. At the beginning of the experiment, he presented the students with a random collection of items: a 1998 bottle of Jaboulet Côtes du Rhône Parallèle 45 wine, a 1996 bottle of Jaboulet Hermitage La Chapelle wine, a cordless trackball, a cordless keyboard and mouse, a design book, and a one-pound box of Belgian chocolates.

Next, he handed out a form listing the items to each student and told them to write the last two digits of their social security number, in the form of a price, next to each of the items. For example, let's pretend the last two digits of my social security number are seven and four; in that case,

I would've written $74 next to each item. Then he asked the students to indicate on the form whether or not they would be willing to pay that price for each item. Lastly, the students were asked to write down the maximum amount they would be willing to spend for each item.

After collecting the forms, Ariely analyzed the data, looking for any correlation between the two-digit numbers and the amount the students had estimated they would be willing to spend.

He discovered that the students that started with higher two-digit social security numbers bid highest, while those with the lower numbers bid lowest. Remarkably, those with two-digit numbers in the upper 20% placed bids that were *216–346% higher* than those of the students with Social Security numbers ending in the lowest 20%.[125]

Think about that.

A completely arbitrary number, wholly unrelated to the items at issue, impacted the students' perception of value by a factor of three. Still think that random and unrelated factors do not influence our perception of value?

Ariely's bidding experiment highlights the influence of one of the most stubborn ghosts in the machine: *anchoring*.

ANCHORING

Anchoring is a cognitive bias that leads individuals to depend too heavily on an initial piece of information offered—that is, an anchor—when making decisions. In the Ariely experiment, each student's two-digit social security number was the anchor.

125   Dan Ariely, *Predictably Irrational: The Hidden Forces That Shape Our Decisions* (New York: HarperCollins, 2008), 28–32.

Anchoring creates reference points, which are a powerful means to frame decision-making that you will recall from our prospect theory discussion in the previous chapter. In the process of changing their minds, recall that people tend to think in terms of a pre-established status quo when comparing the value of different options.

In this part of the sales cycle, rather than understanding that prospects will be influenced by a pre-established status quo, either your or your negotiating partner will be setting anchors as reference points in real time. Just like the anchor of an actual boat, these cognitive anchors set the value of an item so immovably that all future discussions of that item will pivot around that figure.

Anchors are stubborn. Once they are set, they are difficult to ignore. Adjustments can and will be made, but those adjustments tend to remain closely tethered to the initial anchor. Tversky and Kahneman originally theorized the anchoring-and-adjustment heuristic, illustrating in a number of studies that adjustments are usually insufficient to neutralize the influence of the initial anchor.[126]

Building on this theory, studies show[127] that even when people are made expressly aware of an anchor and offered a monetary reward for a more optimal adjustment, they are still unable to effectively disassociate from an anchor once it has been set. Further, the anchoring phenomenon affects everyone, even those who are highly knowledgeable of the item(s) being discussed.[128]

---

126   See for example Amos Tversky and Daniel Kahneman, "Judgment under Uncertainty: Heuristics and Biases," *Science* 185, no. 4157 (September 1974): 1124–31.

127   Fritz Strack and Thomas Mussweiler, "Explaining the Enigmatic Anchoring Effect: Mechanisms of Selective Accessibility," *Journal of Personality and Social Psychology* 73, no. 3 (1997): 437–46.

128   Birte Englich, Thomas Mussweiler, Fritz Strack, "Playing Dice with Criminal Sentences: The Influence of Irrelevant Anchors on Experts' Judicial Decision Making," *Personality and Social Psychology Bulletin* 32, no. 2 (February 2006): 188–200.

Several theories have been put forth to explain what causes anchoring, but the behavioral science community has yet to reach a consensus. One theory—selective accessibility—proposes that anchors are sticky because they are readily accessible, which makes it more efficient for the brain to measure all subsequent offers or counterpoints against them; this is basically another instance of the availability bias we have already discussed.

Anchors are of particular interest to us in this stage of sales because anchors are typically used to establish a starting point for a negotiation. Contrary to the cliché that you should never make the first offer, being the first to make an offer enables a negotiator to anchor the negotiation around terms that are beneficial to them. As the results from the social security number experiment illustrate, firing the initial shot in a negotiation can have a powerful impact on the subsequent counteroffers that will be made.

While adjustments to the initial anchor are sure to be made over the course of a negotiation, that initial anchor still has a stronger influence on the outcome than the subsequent counteroffers. More to the point, studies suggest that negotiators who set the first offer frequently achieve more economically advantageous results.[129] For these reasons, people around the negotiating table will often compete with one another for the privilege of being the first to set an anchor.

All this being said, anchors are not the only thing to consider for negotiating success, and, while they can confer significant benefits to a specific side, they can also constitute a risk.

---

129   Adam D. Galinsky and Thomas Mussweiler, "First Offers as Anchors: The Role of Perspective-Taking and Negotiator Focus," *Journal of Personality and Social Psychology* 81, no. 4 (2001): 657–69.

If the party setting the initial anchor is unfamiliar with the item or issue being discussed, they risk setting an anchor that is detrimental to their desired outcome. It has also been shown that negotiators who set the first anchor tend to be less satisfied with the outcome of a negotiation than their counter-parties—even if the outcome is economically beneficial to them. This is likely due to disappointment that negotiations have adjusted away from the initial anchor, which likely represented a more optimal outcome for the anchor-setting negotiator.

In addition, the counteroffering party has the advantage of determining the midway point between the initial anchor and their counteroffer, providing them with a measure of control over the ultimate outcome of the negotiation.

Anchors are powerful tools that you can use to successfully navigate a negotiation. However, they need to be wielded with caution and restraint. **Just like the anchor of a boat holds it in place, anchors in our minds can hold us back and keep us from reaching our desired destination.**

Do not race to set an anchor simply because you think it will give you some competitive advantage. If you are not careful, you may inadvertently tie yourself to a less-than-optimal outcome. You also need to be on the lookout for the anchors that your counterparty sets—intentionally or otherwise. These, too, may end up artificially limiting a negotiation's range of possible outcomes.

———

The stubborn ghost of anchoring is a bit more situation-specific and less all-encompassing than the competitive ghost of zero-sum bias, but both make their indelible mark on negotiations. Depending on how you approach them, these ghosts will either help or hinder your efforts to secure a beneficial working relationship with a new customer. Being aware of how these two apparitions affect your and your counterparty's perception of a negotiation—as well as recognizing where a negotiation falls on the spectrum of distributive to integrative—will assist you in leveraging them for the better.

However, if you want to arrive at more optimal solutions in your negotiations, do not try to manipulate the competitive and stubborn ghosts. These ghosts are especially sensitive to manipulation, and they will redouble their interfering efforts if they feel like you are trying to trick them.

Instead, you need to disarm them by letting them know you are in it together.

AMPLIFY YOUR COLLABORATIVE INSTINCTS

"Seek first to understand, then to be understood."
—Stephen Covey

Without further delay, let's revisit the medicinal tree case study that I outlined at the beginning of this chapter.

First, a quick refresher. You—the owner of the trees—have genetically engineered these trees so that the compounds in their roots will assist in the treatment of an otherwise untreatable form of cancer, a cancer to which you are biologically predisposed. You are midway through the trial process, which you must complete if you hope to realize your goal of bringing a treatment to market, but you have run out of money.

You have been approached by another party who is interested in your trees. They also see the potential medicinal properties of the trees—to treat heart disease—and would like to buy the rights to the trees from you. They have offered a reasonable and considerable amount for the trees, but they want full ownership and control, potentially putting an end to your research.

The question you were left with: what do you do?

When my peers in business school were presented with this situation, most of the negotiations concluded with some version of a win-lose outcome. In general, either the current owner kept the trees but found no way to address their need for an injection of capital, or the offering party won the rights to the trees after agreeing to pay some amount of money greater than their initial offer. In either case, both parties approached the negotiation competitively and walked away feeling as though someone had won while the other person had lost.

Although there were dishearteningly few creative solutions beyond these general outcomes, there were a few negotiators who found a win-win solution.

In the post-case debrief discussion—a formal and important part of the case study format—it became clear that, without exception, the negotiators who did find win-win solutions approached the negotiation believing that they could figure out a way for both parties to get what they wanted. That way, it turned out, hinged on one key piece of information that each party knew about their own group but not the other. During the course of the negotiation, unless the parties asked the right questions and probed for a better understanding of the other party's specific needs, these key bits of information remained unknown.

In setting up the case, the instructions given to the

non-owning party explained that they were specifically interested in compounds in the *leaves* of the tree. They were unaware, however, that the owning party had a specific interest in the *roots* of the tree.

Figuring out each other's specific needs during the course of the negotiation proved to be the aha moment that enabled these negotiators to figure out a win-win solution.

The success these negotiators found provides us with a road map that we may use as a guide when we approach negotiations with our prospects. In short, the key to disarming the competitive ghost is to begin a negotiation with the belief that there may be a win-win outcome. This may seem a subtle or unimportant shift in mindset, but it will have ripple effects throughout the process in a variety of ways.

Negotiating with a cooperative mindset does not mean you should let your potential business partners walk all over you. Rather, it simply requires that, before you do anything else, you disarm your counterparty's competitive instincts by actively listening to understand what they want or need to walk away with.

Now, imagine that you are sitting across the negotiation table from a prospect.

Getting to this point in the sales cycle is a testament to your hard work and persistence thus far. The fact that this person has made the decision to work with you and has joined you at the negotiating table is, by any measure, a resounding success. You have every right to be ecstatic that you have made it to this point.

This is the moment the entire sales cycle has been building

toward. You have climbed a mountain, and all that remains between you and the realization of all your effort is to formally solidify your relationship with your soon-to-be-customer. The question facing you now is this: *what will it take to convert this prospect into a paying customer?*

Too often, as the sales cycle shifts into the negotiating stage—where salespeople and prospects need to sit down and hash out the finer points of their mutually desired future working relationship—the goodwill that took so much concerted effort to build vanishes. Suddenly, salesperson and prospect—just like my friends in business school—look across the table and see an opponent rather than the professional friend they have worked with to get this far.

If you look across the negotiating table and see an opponent, your competitive instincts will take over, emboldening the competitive ghosts. Your counterparty will no doubt respond in kind. This is precisely the problem I presented you with earlier in the chapter in the example of the bank versus the private equity firm.

The managing director of the private equity firm—who did not have a relationship with the bank staff to speak of—looked across the table and saw a competitor. In turn, the bank's portfolio manager felt attacked and responded in kind. Once each party's competitive instincts took over, the negotiation was doomed to be distributive, with both sides battling to be the winner of the biggest piece of the pie.

Worse, all the goodwill that had been built over the preceding three years between the bank and the company's management team was now at risk of being permanently lost.

If those executives had been able to look across the negotiating table and recognize a partner, they could instead have let their collaborative instincts take the lead, helping to walk those competitive ghosts back from the ledge that they threatened to career over.

Whether you approach a negotiation competitively or collaboratively makes all the difference.

The negotiators who were able to find a win-win solution to the medicinal tree case understood the importance of collaboration. They approached the negotiation believing they would find a better way if they worked *with* their counterparty, even if they did not know exactly what path they would end up taking. Despite the fact that the case of the tree appears to be a distributive problem, these negotiators looked across the table and recognized a partner—a collaborator with whom they could work to further human health and development.

As we have discussed, most people are led to the negotiating table by the competitive ghost. They expect to see an opponent, and they come locked and loaded, ready for battle. In anticipation of this moment, salespeople and customers alike spend their time and energy preparing to compete over who will win, who will get the biggest slice of pie. In the process, they might be missing the various integrative ways the pie could be shared.

What can salespeople do to disarm the competitive ghosts and amplify their cooperative instincts?

The answer lies in something we discussed in the prospecting chapter: instant gratification. Or rather, pushing back against our need for it.

MARSHMALLOWS AND COOPERATION

As you will recall, procrastination—one of the deceitful ghosts—creates a short-term focus that leads to delay or postponement of effortful action in favor of things that produce a quick burst of satisfaction. This time around, we are interested in delaying our desire for instant gratification, and the selfishness it promotes, through recognition and embrace of the collective good.

Delaying our need for gratification now in order to look forward to future profits is the key that unlocks more collaborative negotiations.

The ability to delay gratification and push back against our innate bias for the present moment is critical for human cooperation. "Winning" a competition, after all, provides a powerful instant gratification. When a group of people strives to achieve a collective goal, the individuals within that group must subordinate their selfish temptations for instant, personal gratification in order to look forward to the benefit of the greater group.

Studies on young children have demonstrated the positive impacts of delayed gratification for decades. The general consensus of these studies is that, no matter their area of focus or interest, the more likely a child is to delay gratification, the greater likelihood they have of achieving success later in life. The most famous of these studies is the Stanford marshmallow experiment.

Led by Stanford psychologist Walter Mischel, the experiment offered individual children a choice between one marshmallow[130] that they could have now—instant

---

130   If the child did not want a marshmallow, they were given the option of a pretzel instead.

gratification—or two marshmallows if they waited for a period of time[131]—delayed gratification. In follow-up studies, the children who had been able to delay their gratification also tended to have better life outcomes, as measured by SAT scores,[132] educational attainment,[133] body mass index (BMI),[134] and other life measures.[135] This is an impressive and powerful finding.[136]

Although insightful, the Stanford Marshmallow Experiment, and others like it, have largely explored delayed gratification from the perspective of an individual. Until recently, very little investigation has been done into the impact of delayed gratification in the context of cooperation.

That changed when, in 2019, assistant professor of psychology Rebecca Koomen and her colleagues at the University of Dundee investigated how a cooperative context would affect the tendency for delayed gratification among pairs of children using a modified version of the marshmallow test.[137] Specifically, they wanted to know whether kids would be more or less likely to delay gratification when relying on one another.

To test this, they ran the marshmallow test with one small

131   15 minutes, in the case of the original study.

132   Walter Mischel, Yuichi Shoda, and Monica L. Rodriguez, "Delay of Gratification in Children," *Science* 244, no. 4907 (May 1989): 933–38.

133   Ozlem N. Ayduk et al., "Regulating the Interpersonal Self: Strategic Self-Regulation for Coping with Rejection Sensitivity," *Journal of Personality and Social Psychology* 79, no. 5 (2000): 776–92.

134   Tanya R. Schlam et al., "Preschoolers' Delay of Gratification Predicts Their Body Mass 30 Years Later," *Journal of Pediatrics* 162, no. 1 (2013): 90–93.

135   Yuichi Shoda, Walter Mischel, and Philip K. Peake, "Predicting Adolescent Cognitive and Self-Regulatory Competencies from Preschool Delay of Gratification: Identifying Diagnostic Conditions," *Developmental Psychology* 26, no. 6 (1990): 978–86.

136   There has been some recent controversy regarding the replicability of the marshmallow test. Other factors, such as children's social environments, are likely to be at least as predictive of the aforementioned life outcomes (SAT scores, education, BMI, etc.) as the capacity for delaying gratification.

137   Rebecca Koomen, Sebastian Grueneisen, and Esther Herrmann, "Children Delay Gratification for Cooperative Ends," *Psychological Science* 31, no. 2 (2020): 139–48.

tweak—using cookies instead of marshmallows—and one large tweak—the children were assigned a partner and told that they both had to delay gratification in order to receive the second cookie. If one of kids ate the first cookie before allotted time expired, neither would receive a second. The children would need to collaborate if they wanted to double down on their treats. As a control, the researchers also ran the updated test without making the reward of the second cookie dependent on the performance of a partner, effectively replicating the original, individually focused marshmallow test.

The results of this updated marshmallow test are a definitive win for the power of collaboration. The researchers found that 48.6% of the children who were dependent on one another waited until the allotted time expired before eating their cookie, successfully delaying their gratification. For those children who were not dependent on one another, only 26.5% waited. In other words, structuring the experiment as a collaborative game resulted in an 85% increase in delayed gratification, which in turn was the key to unlocking more optimal outcomes.

While there have not yet been studies replicating these results in adults or generalizing them to other scenarios, these outcomes still speak to the human animal's collaborative instincts, which are all too often disregarded or ignored in the context of negotiating. This is the first half of the equation that the successful negotiators in the medicinal tree case understood: **finding ways to leverage our instinct for collaboration is the path of least resistance for salespeople interested in disarming the competitive ghost**.

UNDERSTANDING INTERESTS

As a salesperson, if you want to prevent the prospect on the other side of the table from seeing you as an enemy combatant, you would do well to frame the negotiation as something that the two of you are tackling together— which is true. You want to make the sale, and they have already decided that they want your product or service. You *are* partners. You *are* dependent on each other. What you are not is enemies out to defeat each other. (I leave it up to you whether or not to incorporate marshmallows or cookies.)

Even if you know that the negotiation game you are playing is an especially distributive one, as a salesperson, you are still a partner to the party sitting across from you at the negotiating table; you still want to have a long-term working relationship with them. Even in distributive negotiations, there will always be ways for you to engender a spirt of collaboration throughout the course of a negotiation.

One of the best ways to promote collaboration between negotiating parties is to "seek first to understand."[138]

This is the other half of the equation that drove the successful parties in the medicinal tree case. Being sincerely interested in understanding what the other party wanted and needed motivated the successful negotiators to ask questions that uncovered what was hiding just beneath the surface—the specific need each party had for different parts of the tree.

Once again, the importance of being a good listener cannot be overstated as a key to success in negotiating

---

138   Stephen R. Covey, *The 7 Habits of Highly Effective People* (New York: Free Press, 1989).

and sales (and life, for that matter). Listening may not seem like a decisive action to start a negotiation with, and it may be the last thing your competitive instincts want to do. However, while listening may be subtle, it is a powerful tool.

It is not a coincidence that active listening is the same solution we discussed in the relationship building chapter. Active listening enables you to better connect with your prospects and customers, and it can ultimately lead toward a less combative and competitive relationship—a relationship where they will be able to let down their guard and give you information about what they really want. You, in turn, will be better able to find creative solutions that satisfy both parties.

Once a negotiation begins, the stubborn ghost will encourage each party to dig their heels in and resist ceding any ground from the positions to which they are anchored. Moving the focus of the negotiation *away* from those positions is critical to disarming the stubborn ghost and finding more optimal solutions.

As Roger Fisher and William Ury discuss in their best-selling book *Getting to Yes*—arguably the best negotiations book ever written—focusing on *interest* rather than *positions* shifts the focus of the negotiation squarely onto the problem at hand.

Underneath any given position is a desire or need. For example, a negotiating party may state that they want to sell their house for one million dollars. This is their position. But what they really need is enough money to settle their debts and afford a down payment for their next house—this is their interest.

As Fisher and Ury note in their book, focusing on interests is more effective than digging in on positions for two reasons. One, "...for every interest there usually exists several possible positions that could satisfy it." And, two, "Behind opposed positions lie shared and compatible interests...."[139] In other words, focusing on underlying interests promotes flexibility and creativity in negotiating while simultaneously assisting both parties in recognizing all the ways their interests might already be aligned.

If you take away nothing else from this chapter, remember this: focusing on positions provokes win-lose solutions. Focusing on interests facilitates win-win solutions.

This was another fundamental flaw in the renegotiation between the bank and the private equity firm. Both sides were focused on positions, not interests. The private equity firm's position was that the bank should step up and fix the problem with an extension of credit. The bank's position was that this was an equity problem that should not be fixed with debt.

These positions created a black-and-white perception of the possible outcome of the negotiation. Either the private equity firm's position would carry the day and the bank would provide additional credit, or the bank's position would win out and the private equity firm would prop the company up with an equity injection.

Blinded by commitment to their respective positions, neither side could see any possible alternatives. In reality, their respective interests—the drivers underneath these specific positions—were more aligned than expected, yet neither side was willing to consider those interests at the time.

---

139   Roger Fisher, William Ury, and Bruce Patton, *Getting to Yes: Negotiating Agreement without Giving In*, 2nd ed. (New York: Penguin, 1991), 42.

Fortunately, on a follow-up call a few days later, cooler heads prevailed.

During this call, the two sides were able to move past their stated positions and come to a better understanding of each other's interests. The managing director of the private equity firm was hesitant to commit equity because it would reflect poorly on his leadership in the eyes of his investors and dilute his management team's equity interest in the company. Conversely, the bank did not really need additional equity to be put into the company; rather, it was unable to extend additional credit without collateral support or a guarantee from the private equity firm.

Based on these interests, the two sides were able to find a creative solution that would satisfy their respective interests. The bank would provide the company with a two-million-dollar line of credit backed by a guarantee from the private equity firm, which provided the bank with a means to recoup its investment in the company in the event the additional money was not repaid. The private equity firm got what they needed, and the bank, once again, was able to step up for the company. Both sides stopped playing the proverbial game of financial chicken, averting a crisis by focusing on interests rather than positions, and everybody won.

Whether in the sterile environs of academia or the nitty-gritty of the real world, framing your negotiation as a collaborative effort and listening to understand in order to focus on interests, rather than positions, are the two major keys to disarming the competitive and stubborn ghosts. These tools can shift the discussion away from a win-lose approach and ultimately provide the groundwork for more optimal negotiated outcomes.

Understanding this, there is just one more thing a salesperson needs to do in order be a more successful negotiator, and it is the most effective tool of all: be prepared.

BE PREPARED

"Failing to prepare is preparing to fail."
—Unknown

If you do nothing else, simply understanding the pull of the competitive and stubborn ghosts—for both your prospect and yourself—will lead you to lean in to collaboration and focus on one another's interests, which will carry you most of the way toward realizing more optimal outcomes. However, if you want replicable and consistent success at the negotiating table, you need to do some homework before the negotiation begins.

Negotiations can get complicated in a hurry, and it is difficult to keep everything straight if you only rely on what you can keep track of in your head. Even negotiations that seem simple and straightforward can quickly get lost in a maze of tangential issues if you are not careful and disciplined in maintaining focus on the issues you sat down to negotiate in the first place; getting lost in these details can make it much easier to give in to your natural competitive instincts and lose your sense of cooperation and your ability to listen.

The best way to set yourself up for success in any given negotiation is to prepare in advance.

Clichéd as it may be, "failing to prepare is preparing to fail" most certainly applies in a negotiation context. Experience is a wonderful teacher and will hone instincts that are otherwise hard to teach, but I would argue that preparation is even more important than experience, at least in the context of negotiating. Preparing yourself with the facts and figures will help lay the groundwork for reframing the discussion and thinking of creative ways to share the pie.

Getting good at preparation does not require having been in hundreds or thousands of negotiations. And preparing sufficiently for a negotiation is a decidedly simple exercise. It need not take hours. It is more like a thorough conversation with a partner or colleague than it is a mentally exhausting homework exercise.

What follows is a guide that will help facilitate that conversation—even if you are only having it with yourself.

I present the official GitM Negotiation Cheat Sheet. All you need to do is fill in the blanks, and you will be well on your way to successfully navigating your way toward more optimal negotiated outcomes.

Official **GitM** Cheat Sheet

What type of negotiation is this, distributive or integrative?

- What are the distributive and integrative aspects of the negotiation?

How will you frame the negotiation as a collaborative effort?

- What is a theme that unites the negotiating parties?

What is your target agreement?

- Your target agreement is the ideal outcome from your perspective.

What is your counter party's target agreement?

- If you do not know, make your best assumption.

What is your best alternative to negotiated agreement (BATNA)?

- What are your alternatives if the negotiation reaches an impasse?

What is your reservation agreement?

- The reservation agreement is the worst offer you're willing to accept.
- DO NOT reveal this to the other party.

What is your counter party's reservation agreement?

- If you do not know, make your best assumption.

What is the zone of possible agreement (ZOPA)?

- This is the range between each party's reservation agreement.

What are your sources of power?

- What advantages do you have over your counter party?
- If you do not know, make your best assumption.

What are their sources of power?

- If you do not know, make your best assumption.

Preparing in advance of a negotiation—whether you use this cheat sheet or not—is important because it is a way to mitigate your own emotional instincts and reactions over the course of a negotiation. Remember—it is not only your counterparty who is subject to the influence of the competitive and stubborn ghosts.

Outlining what is most important to you, things you are willing to concede, and the various ways you may find win-win outcomes, all *before* your competitive juices start flowing and you have anchored yourself to a handful of positions, will typically establish a more rational approach that will serve you better than those baser instincts. Although you are not a perfectly rational *Homo economicus*, preparation will help you better mimic one, and, for the purposes of negotiation, that is a very good thing.

Although I encourage you to bring this cheat sheet with you to use as a beacon while you are negotiating, just the process of preparing this cheat sheet, going through the motions of thinking through these variables, will provide you with solid grounding that will help you keep the negotiation on track and headed toward an optimal outcome.

No one can promise you a trick to get exactly what you want out of a given negotiation, but I will promise that using this GitM cheat sheet will be a huge leap forward in successfully navigating your negotiations—not to mention giving your newly minted customer a good feeling about your future working together.

BONUS: FAIRNESS AND SATISFICING

Thanks to our beneficial evolutionarily pull toward cooperation, there are a handful of universal beliefs held by people throughout the world—beliefs that connect all human beings, regardless of culture, color, or creed. In global surveys about what they believe is paramount for a good life, people consistently highlight things like happiness, good health, time spent with family, and safety. Additionally—and perhaps above all else—people express an expectation and desire to be treated fairly.

FAIRNESS

Fairness refers to our social preference for equitable outcomes.[140] Fairness is foundational to the social norm of reciprocity—the obligation to return favors and/or gifts—and one of the six key factors of influence identified by persuasion specialist Robert Cialdini (along with liking, which we discussed in Relationship Building).[141] In the field of behavioral science, this common desire for fairness is formally known as the universal ethic of reciprocity.

THE UNIVERSAL ETHIC OF RECIPROCITY

In The Social Leap, von Hippel reintroduces the concept of fairness in the context of Homo sapiens' broader evolution toward cooperation. In short, as soon as it became evolutionarily advantageous for human beings to be more social, two things quickly rose to the surface as critically important.

- Fairness took on a moral authority.
- Freeloading became the greatest challenge to community survival.

According to von Hippel's theory, in a cooperation-based

140   "Fairness," *Behavorialeconomics.com*, https://www.behavioraleconomics.com/resources/mini-encyclopedia-of-be/fairness/#:~:text=In%20behavioral%20science%2C%20fairness%20refers,own%20or%20someone%20else's%20favor.
141   Robert B. Cialdini, *Influence: The Psychology of Persuasion* (New York: HarperCollins, 2007).

society, while fairness rises to the level of a moral precept as the glue that holds the group together, free-riding sinks to the level of immorality. Individuals who skip out on contributing their fair share while reaping the same reward as everyone else could pose an existential threat to the entire community.

In this framework, lying, cheating, and stealing are universally reviled across cultures because each is viewed as being uncooperative and, therefore, unfair.

- *The liar deceives others to their own benefit.*
- *The cheater accomplishes their deeds by leeching off the work of others.*
- *The thief takes from another what they did not earn themselves.*

So serious were these issues to our ancestors that liars, cheats, and thieves were threatened with ostracism from the group–an effective death sentence for an individual left to fend for themselves on the open plains of the savanna.[142]

The life-and-death tension between cooperation and freeloading underpins the moral authority of fairness and the universal ethic of reciprocity, which has been one of the principal teachings of the world's religions for millennia—most frequently appearing as a version of the Golden Rule: do unto others as you would have them do unto you.

Fairness is at the very heart of our species' ability to survive and thrive. At the end of the day, we are all in this together. The sun rises and shines on everyone the same. We all breathe the same air. And we, people all over the

142   William von Hippel, *The Social Leap: The New Evolutionary Science of Who We Are, Where We Come From, and What Makes Us Happy* (New York: HarperCollins, 2018).

planet, people of all different shapes and sizes and colors, all have the same fundamental needs and desires, including the desire to be treated fairly.

Therefore, treating your prospects fairly is basic table stakes in negotiating. If your prospects or customers view a negotiation as unfair—whether or not the situation is necessarily competitive—it will be difficult for them to consider anything else until fairness has been restored.

As a matter of fact, perhaps we should behaviorally tweak the Golden Rule. Rather than "do unto others as *you* would have them to do unto you," I suggest you strive to "do unto others as *they* would have you do unto them."

This slight tweak will nudge you toward embracing the negotiation through your counterparty's frame of reference, increasing the likelihood that you will be perceived as cooperative, understanding of their circumstances, and, ultimately, fair. All of which will increase the odds that you will be able to steer a negotiation toward a more optimal outcome for yourself as well.

SATISFICING

Most people, most of the time, do *not* strive to maximize their outcomes. Instead, people usually settle for good enough. This is the essence of *satisficing*, and your prospects and customers do it constantly.

Satisficing is a portmanteau of *satisfy* and *suffice* introduced to the behavioral science community by Herbert A. Simon, the same gentleman who brought us bounded rationality. In his Nobel prize acceptance speech, Simon described his logic thusly: "Decision-makers can satisfice either by finding optimum solutions for a simplified world, or by finding satisfactory solutions for a more realistic world."[143] Satisficing is an approach to decision-making that involves finding an outcome that is acceptable—not perfect.

What is the takeaway for the negotiating salesperson? Your goal does not need to be to find a perfect solution. And a perfect solution is probably not your prospect's goal, either.

In the real world, especially in the context of negotiating, perfect solutions are few and far between. Instead, seek out *better* solutions, solutions that are satisficing for both you and your counterparty.

———

Negotiating is far from the esoteric exercise that many consider it to be.

Like most things in life—including the various stages of the sales cycle that we are discussing in this book—being a successful negotiator simply comes down to understanding and executing a few key principles. With the insight and tools provided in this chapter, you have everything you need to approach any given negotiation with confidence and the expectation of success.

I cannot emphasize enough the importance of seeking out ways to frame your negotiation as collaborative.

Do not assume yours is a win-lose situation. Taking an integrative approach, even if your negotiation is mostly distributive, can only positively impact your outcomes. **If you can find ways to align yourself with your counterparty and**

---

143   Herbert A. Simon, "Rational Decision-Making in Business Organizations," (Nobel Memorial Lecture, December 8, 1978), 350.

steer the conversation toward your respective interests, rather than becoming anchored to your stated positions, you will successfully disarm the competitive and stubborn ghosts and find your way to an outcome that meets your goals as well as those of your prospect.

As we have discussed over the course of the last two chapters, what many consider "selling" is really a combination of changing and negotiating. In fact, per the behavioral science principles we have become familiar with as this journey has unfolded, very little "selling"—as those outside of sales perceive it—actually happens in the sales cycle. I believe the understanding put forth in this and the previous chapter provides a clearer view of what professional salespeople need to do in order to realize sustainable success.

And, as we move past both changing and negotiating, sustaining success is exactly what we are going to talk about in the next chapter.

GROWING

Once there was a king. He was the wisest and strongest king this world had ever seen.

He ruled over the biggest and most prosperous city in the world. He cleared huge fields so that his people could cultivate the land and be prosperous. He built glorious towers so that his people would be able to worship him. He surrounded the city with a great wall to protect his people.

He was a great king. But he was also arrogant and cruel.

He enslaved his people in order to realize his great fields, towers, and walls. And he threatened to kill anyone who defied him.

With his best friend at his side, he ruled his world absolutely, slaying all the mythical beasts and demons that came to challenge his control of the world.

Displeased with the king's arrogance and cruelty, as punishment, the gods struck down his best friend with a grave illness, and he died a few days later. Filled with sorrow, and feeling rejected by the gods, the king fell into a deep depression. He abandoned his city to wander the wilderness in mourning for his friend.

While mourning and contemplating the fragility of life, he came to believe that his life's purpose was to find a cure for death and live forever. So the king set out on a journey to find the only man in the world whom the gods had blessed with the gift of immortality.

On his journey to find the immortal man, the king was confronted with a variety of trials, tests of his worth. These trials, it seemed, were designed to challenge the king in ways that targeted his greatest weaknesses—his arrogance and cruelty. Along the way he was pushed to his very limit, and there came a moment when, for the first time in his life, the king failed. All hope seemed lost.

Then, at the darkest moment, a stranger offered the king a clue that would help him find what he sought. Renewed, and grateful for the stranger's kindness, the king went on to discover the secret to immortality.

After securing his prize, he made his way back home to prove his righteousness to the gods. Yet one night, just as he was on the verge of making his triumphant return, the king's prize was stolen. After everything he had experienced on his journey, he would be coming home empty-handed.

Upon his return, as he made his way through the gates of the great wall, he looked upon the city he had known his whole life—the city he'd built with his arrogance and cruelty—with a different perspective. For the first time he recognized the vibrance of its inhabitants: everyone connected through a delicate and inclusive web that would live on long after he was dead and gone.

For the first time in his life, the king came to terms with his mortality. *Individuals may not be immortal*, he thought, *but humanity is*. He realized that life will always find a way to survive and thrive, even in the face an arrogant and cruel king.

From that day on the king let go of his arrogant and cruel ways, and led his people with empathy and caring. And—dare I say—everyone lived happily ever after.

THE OLDEST STORY EVER TOLD

This story probably sounds familiar. In fact, it is more than likely that you were required to read about this king in school at some point. Written more than four thousand years ago, this is the oldest story ever recorded and (arguably) the first hero epic that human beings ever told each other.

Those readers who recall learning about the cradle of civilization in ancient Mesopotamia will recognize the king as ruler of the Sumerian city of Uruk, and the story as the *Epic of Gilgamesh*. However, this story will sound familiar even to those who have never heard of King Gilgamesh or the epic poem named after him.

You will recognize the same story arc in many kinds of ancient mythology, such as Homer's *Odyssey*, *Jason and the Golden Fleece*, and the story of Prometheus. You will recognize elements from it in countless popular movies, like *The Matrix*, *Star Wars*, *Harry Potter*, and *Finding Nemo*.

And you will even recognize it in the origin stories of the principal figures of the world's three monotheistic religions.

The characters, location, and events of the hero epic change depending on who is telling the story and when it is being told, but the story always remains the same: The hero embarks on a journey to discover something. Along the way, the hero is faced with challenges they must overcome. Overcoming the challenges affects a change in the hero. The hero returns home a better version of themselves and shares what they have learned with the world.

This universal story arc is known as *the hero's journey*, and it is humanity's favorite story.

THE HERO'S JOURNEY

Common patterns in the plots of hero epics across cultures have been recognized since the late 1800s, but the concept of the hero's journey as it is known today was popularized by Joseph Campbell in his 1949 masterpiece The Hero with a Thousand Faces.[144]

In the book, as well as in subsequent teachings and lectures, Campbell uses the universality of the hero's journey to deconstruct and compare a wide variety of myths and religious teachings. He identifies the three main acts—like the acts of a play—that are consistently represented in each hero's journey:

- *The Departure*

  The hero receives a call to depart from the ordinary world and go on an adventure. The hero may willingly accept the call or may be drawn into the adventure by uncontrollable circumstances—just

144   Joseph Campbell, *The Hero with a Thousand Faces* (New York: Pantheon, 1949).

as Gilgamesh was drawn into the search for immortality while mourning the loss of his friend.

- **The Initiation**

  The hero faces tasks or trials and is eventually confronted with the central crisis of the adventure. In the initiation, the hero must overcome this final obstacle and learn the necessary lesson in order to be transformed—just as Gilgamesh had to let go of his search for immortality in order to recognize it in the people of his city.

- **The Return**

  The hero must then return to the ordinary world with this new understanding and use it for the benefit of his fellow man—just as Gilgamesh learned the error of his arrogance and cruelty and embraced empathy and caring.

Although each act is integral to the story, the key moment in every version of the hero's journey happens during the initiation, when the hero embraces a final transformation. No matter the prelude to this transformation, the hero will always be defined by their willingness to let go of the old and embrace the new. In a very fundamental way, the hero's journey is about evolving and adapting—growing.

If you are wondering how the hero's journey relates to our journey through the sales cycle, hold that thought and consider this: just like the heroes of ancient mythology, real-life heroes must also embrace growth.

Roger Federer, perhaps the greatest tennis player to ever live, was not always the smooth and gentlemanly competitor that the world knows and loves today. Growing up, and even into his first few years as a professional, he was just as well known for throwing rackets, screaming, and cursing during matches as he was for his undeniable abilities on the court.

When asked to reflect on his career and the secret to his success, he had this to say:

> I can't stand it, watching me throwing rackets and embarrass myself in front of thousands of people in a live stadium. So I tried to change. [I] had quite a transformation from a screaming, racket-throwing, swearing kind of brat on the tennis court to this calm guy today. It's very important to sort of move on. And I think also losses make you stronger. It's important to learn out of those mistakes and then you become better and the better player, you work harder.[145]

Even after he had mastered control of his emotional outbursts and established himself as the dominant force in men's tennis, maintaining an ironclad grip on the number one ranking for a record 237 consecutive weeks—more than four and a half years!—Mr. Federer never stopped seeking out ways to improve.

> I always questioned myself in the best of times... at certain times during the year I said, "What can I improve? What do I need to change?" Because if you don't do anything or you just do the same thing over and over again, you stay the same, and staying the same means going backwards.[146]

---

145 "Roger Federer—Give Your Best," Goalcast, April 3, 2017, https://www.goalcast.com/2017/04/03/roger-federer-never-stop-improving/.
146 "Roger Federer," Goalcast.

The things Roger Federer has accomplished on the tennis court are unquestionably heroic, but I maintain that this is not what makes him a hero. He is a hero because in his life, time and time again, he has come to the point of transformation—and each time, he has shown a willingness to let go of the old and embrace the new: evolving, adapting, growing.

Good news: being a hero is not reserved only for kings, or for those who achieve fantastic athletic success.

Over the course of our lives, each and every one of us is presented with multiple opportunities for transformation. **At each of these moments, we can choose to reject change and retreat back to safety—or we can choose to embrace it and move forward toward growth.**

These are the choices that determine whether or not we become the heroes of our own stories—and, in many cases, the choices that determine whether we will move forward and grow our careers or stagnate at a plateau. Choose wisely.

If you have made it to this point—looking ahead at what needs to be done to build a sustainable sales growth engine—then you have successfully navigated the ghostly gauntlet that is the sales cycle, which is no small feat. Congratulations are in order. It is time to give yourself some credit, to feel some well-earned satisfaction.

And once you have acknowledged your progress and rewarded yourself in a way you feel is appropriate, it is time to think about the next time you go through the sales cycle. And the next time. And the next.

We have largely spent this book examining ghosts from

the perspective of how they affect our prospects and customers, but once again, it is time to remember that we are not exempt. Those same ghosts haunt our own minds, and in this chapter, we are going to take a look at a few evolutionary apparitions that can hold us back when it comes to growing and changing.

And so, just as we did at the start of our journey, here, at the end, we are again going to turn the behavioral spotlight back onto *you*.

BE A SALES HERO

*"One can choose to go back toward safety
or forward toward growth."*
—*Abraham Maslow*

Sales is the most important function in any company.

Yes, every function within a company is important. And, yes, no company will achieve its potential unless all internal systems and players perform well. We must acknowledge the contribution of everybody on the team.

However, that said, the company would not exist if not for the sales function. And other systems and players would have nothing to perform if not for someone going out and finding customers who are interested in purchasing the company's products or services—which is the sales function, no matter whether the person doing the finding carries a formal sales title or not.

I am, of course, biased, but I will argue all day long that having an effective sales function is the most critical factor to a company's success. To my mind, there are three reasons this is true.

- Sales keeps the spirit of entrepreneurship alive.
  - By taking an active, boots-on-the-ground role in the marketplace, constantly seeking out new, different, and better ways to market a company's products or services, the sales function keeps the spirit of entrepreneurship alive in businesses large and small, new and old, global and local. And entrepreneurship is the lifeblood of all companies.
- Sales is the most important link between customer and company.
  - Recall from our relationship-building discussion that, beyond affecting purchasing decisions, salespeople are usually the first to connect with prospects and customers. Without salespeople making a good first impression, nobody else at the company will have a chance to make any kind of impression.
  - Some may argue that customer service and account management roles are as important in connecting a company to its customers as pure sales roles. And they are correct. However, I would frame customer service and account management as post-purchase sales roles and argue that their most important function is to encourage customers to continue buying products and services from the company—that is, customer service and account management are salespeople, too.
- Sales is the engine of company growth.
  - At the risk of sounding repetitive, without an active and steady supply of new customers to serve, a business cannot sustain itself.

For these reasons and many more, I do not think it is hyperbole to say that sales professionals may be seen as company heroes.[147]

For a sales function to be truly effective—for it to keep the spirit of entrepreneurship alive, maintain a strong link between customer and company, and serve as a powerful engine of growth—it must have salespeople who embrace their roles as heroes. Specifically, as we learned from the hero's journey, sales heroes must seek out and embrace opportunities for growth.

For the sales hero, growth is a twofold message.

First, like all heroes, we as salespeople must embrace the personal growth that comes from overcoming obstacles through transformation and change, from letting go of the old and embracing the new. As tennis hero Roger Federer said, "if you don't do anything or you just do the same thing over and over again, you stay the same..."

In other words, if you do not change, if you do not embrace new ways of doing things that are better than the old ways, you are going to keep getting the same results. Even if you are one of the few salespeople whose results are already impressive, the only way to keep growing and beat your own record is to continue to change and build on what you have learned.

Second, and more specific to the goal of growing our business, we salespeople need to continue to grow our customer base. Personal growth fuels this goal, but at the end of the day, you are going to want measurable portfolio

---

147   To be fair, everyone working in a company may be seen as a hero, and the more people that choose to actively play this role, the better a company will function overall.

growth as well. And if you want to achieve your business growth goals, you—like all heroes—are going to need a little help.

One of the more underappreciated—yet consistently represented—components of the hero's journey is the help the hero receives along their way. After they have accepted the call to adventure, a guide or magical helper will present themselves to the hero. Sometimes help will come from a stranger, as it did for Gilgamesh, and other times it will come from a mentor figure. In the Odyssey, Athena assisted Odysseus throughout, often disguised as his old friend Mentor (yes, that is seriously his name). In the Matrix, Neo had Morpheus. In Star Wars, Luke had Obi Wan. In Harry Potter, Harry had Dumbledore.

In many of these tales, the hero's choice to embrace the assistance they are offered along the way is the very thing that enables the hero to successfully realize the transformation or change they seek. Similarly, to grow most effectively and efficiently, salespeople must embrace the idea of getting help from those around them, both colleagues and customers.

In general, accepting help from those around you, whether in the form of tips and suggestions, assistance with tasks, or even constructive criticism, leads to personal growth, which will ultimately improve both your work and all areas of life. Although accepting help can be difficult at times— especially given the common perception that accepting help is an implicit admission that we are not capable or good enough on our own—it can boost performance in many ways throughout a sales career, and we would all do well to keep our minds open to help of any kind.

That said, when it comes to growing your sales business, there is one specific kind of help that can boost your portfolio more than any other: referrals.

Growing a sales business, as we discussed in Prospecting, begins with establishing and maintaining a sales funnel full of prospects who are likely to be interested in what you are selling. However, if salespeople hope to consistently and sustainably achieve their business growth goals, prospecting for business via cold calls is not enough. When it comes to accelerating portfolio growth, referrals are the golden ticket.

Where our prospecting discussion focused on cold calling to create consistent opportunities for progress, in seeking to accelerate progress and regularly reach our growth goals, we will now turn our attention to warm calling and all the opportunities for growth it affords.

WARM CALLING

A warm call, as we defined in Prospecting, is one in which an introduction has been made for you via a referral—a "fast-pass" to the in-group we discussed in Relationship Building. Warm calls are the best kind of help when it comes to growing a sales portfolio. Salespeople must consistently execute a well-developed cold-calling strategy if they hope to sustain long-term success, but when it comes to accelerating growth, warm calls are where it's at.

Per Heinz Marketing, 87% of frontline sales reps, 82% of sales leaders, and 78% of marketers agree that referrals are the best leads your business can get.[148] They are

---

148   Jim Williams, "Infographic: 17 B2B Referral Statistics You Should Know (But Probably Don't)," Influitive, December 15, 2015, https://influitive.com/blog/infographic-17-stats-about-b2b-referrals-you-should-know-but-probably-dont/.

> *worth their weight in gold, and most salespeople will tell you that they would kill to have more referrals.*
>
> - *Per to the International Data Corporation (IDC), 73% of executives prefer to work with salespeople who have been referred to them.[149]*
>
> - *A study from the Journal of Marketing showed that referred customers are 16–25% more profitable than other customers.[150]*
>
> - *Data gathered by Mention Me, a referral technology platform, shows that referral campaigns typically experience between a 10–30% increase in customer acquisition.[151]*

Again, cold calling is absolutely vital to your success in sales. Salespeople who purely focus on an effective cold-calling strategy are certain to achieve steady, incremental growth. **However, if you want to consistently and sustainably realize year-after-year growth of 10–30%, you must also leverage an effective warm-calling strategy to complement your cold-calling efforts.**

I appreciate that telling you to leverage referrals may sound like stating the obvious—because it is. And yet, despite the obviousness of this concept, the overwhelming majority of salespeople do *not* have an effective warm-calling strategy.

Worse, they hardly even ask for referrals at all.

- According to a survey by the Sales Insights Lab,

---

149   Kathleen Schaub, *Social Buying Meets Social Selling: How Trusted Networks Improve the Purchase Experience*, International Data Corporation, April 2014.

150   Philipp Schmitt, Bernd Skiera, and Christophe Van den Bulte, "Referral Programs and Customer Value," *Journal of Marketing* 75, no. 1 (January 2011): 46–59.

151   Angela Southall, "How to Make Referral a Great Marketing Channel in Fashion," Mention Me, May 26, 2016, https://www.mention-me.com/blog/how-to-make-referral-marketing-a-channel-in-fashion.

57.9% of respondents said they ask for fewer than 1 referral each month, 40.4% report rarely asking, and only 18.6% ask every client for a referral.[152]

- In a survey by Texas Tech University, 83% of consumers express willingness to provide a referral after a positive experience, but only 29% will volunteer to provide one without being prompted.[153]

The proven effectiveness of referrals, coupled with the lack of focus on asking for them, practically begs the question: if referrals are the key to accelerating growth and sustaining success, why on earth aren't more salespeople prioritizing them? Why do salespeople persistently disregard one of the best tools at their disposal for realizing their full professional potential?

The answer, honestly, is that we are all just a little too high on ourselves.

To better understand why, let's take a quick detour through the history of behavioral science.

FROM FREUD TO KAHNEMAN

"The ego is the single biggest obstruction to the achievement of anything."
—*Richard Rose*

Since its rudimentary beginnings in the late nineteenth century, behavioral science has been focused on understanding why people do what they do. The early founders of the

152   Marc Wayshak, "18 New Sales Statistics for 2020 from Our Groundbreaking Study!," Sales Insights Lab, March 12, 2020, https://salesinsightslab.com/sales-research/.
153   Daniel Decker, "How to Close the Referral Gap," Spotlight Branding, April 9, 2018, https://spotlightbranding.com/close-referral-gap-2/.

field of psychology were generally concerned with either identifying the structures of the mind or exploring how the unconscious mind helps us navigate our environment, with an emphasis on the mind's influence on behavior. These pioneers recognized that behavior is not what it seems on the surface and focused their research techniques on the psychological underpinnings of behavior.

The most well-known of these pioneering figures, Sigmund Freud—aka the godfather of clinical psychology—is largely responsible for the broad structure of our contemporary experience of a visit to the psychologist. You know, the one in which the patient sits or lies on a couch and engages in a discussion of whatever it is that may be bothering them.

Although many of Freud's ideas have not weathered the test of time so well—namely the Oedipus complex, the degree to which sexual energies underlie repressed thoughts and emotions, and the universal benefits of cocaine—he remains a towering figure in the world of behavioral science, and many of the concepts he developed remain stuck in the public consciousness (more on these in a bit).

In the first half of the twentieth century, behaviorists like John B. Watson and B. F. Skinner challenged their prede-cessors' approach on the grounds that mental processes could not be directly observed, and, therefore, focused their efforts on the effects of environmental stimuli upon behavior, which could be observed. In large part, the behaviorists built off Ivan Pavlov's experiments, the most famous of which was his work with dogs on conditioning.

While Freud and his followers looked for truth in the uncon-scious, behaviorists found truth in stimulus and response.

In the middle of the twentieth century, the focus of

behavioral science shifted yet again. Cognitive psychology—in what is sometimes referred to as the "cognitive revolution"—made its way to the stage, focusing on thought, language, problem-solving, and other thought processes and behaviors that could not simply be explained by the interaction between environmental stimuli and behavioral response. This is the school of thought to which many of the behavioral scientists we have met along our journey belong, including Kahneman and Tversky.

The cognitive approach shines the spotlight back on the mind and mental processes that affect behavior, but now it is armed with modern scientific research methods to which those pioneering psychologists did not have access. Coupled with a deeper appreciation for evolutionary influences on behavior, the cognitive view of behavioral science has been our primary guide on our journey through the sales cycle, helping us to better understand all those irrationalities in decision-making driven by the ghosts in the machine.

You may be wondering, "What does all this have to do with growing my sales career and asking for referrals?"

Glad you asked.

Now that we have completed our tour through the history of behavioral science, we can come back to the question that we asked at the end of the previous section: *Why do salespeople persistently disregard referrals as one of the best tools at their disposal for realizing their full professional potential?*

To answer this question, we will first make a nod to Freud, who developed the psychoanalytic concepts of the id, ego, and superego.

According to Freud, these three theoretical constructs describe the mental life of a human being. The id represents a person's primal instincts; the superego represents an individual's view of the socially acceptable standards that they ought to be paying attention to; and the ego is the mental agent that mediates between these two extremes. The ego, as Freud taught, represents the portion of the human personality we popularly identify with the conscious self.

Fast-forward to the present and most psychologists consider the concepts of id, ego, and superego as outdated and unsupported by scientific evidence. However, the term has contributed to the psychological zeitgeist, and it still informs our current understanding of human behavior. **Case in point: based on insights from cognitive psychology, social psychology, and contemporary behavioral science, we now describe humanity as *egocentric*—at least in terms of how we think.**

Painting with broad strokes, to be egocentric is to over-rely on one's own perspective, to be self-centered, and to underestimate—if not completely ignore—other people's point of view.

It is not necessarily that we have an "ego" that mediates between our primal instincts and what is socially acceptable; instead, we simply have a tendency to think mostly of ourselves and have blinders on toward what others might think. And, although I am no Freud, I think it is fair to say that everyone falls somewhere on the egocentric spectrum.

Though it may not be particularly noteworthy or surprising to say that people are self-centered, acknowledging this fact is the key to understanding why salespeople do not do everything in their power to embrace growth and better leverage referrals.

SALESPEOPLE ARE SELF-CENTERED (JUST LIKE EVERYONE ELSE)

*"You are never strong enough that
you don't need help."*
—Cesar Chavez

Because salespeople, like all people, are self-centered and over-reliant on our own perspective, we tend to feel as though life's spotlight is shining down on us—which you will recall as the spotlight effect from our discussion about listening in Relationship Building. **As such, we discount what others think or have to say, disregarding the fact that most opportunities for growth and change come from others' perspectives.**

From our position at the center of the universe, we often consider the experiences of others as inferior to our own, get annoyed at criticism or feedback we feel we do not need, and expect that we should be self-reliant. This self-centered perspective prevents salespeople from recognizing that perspectives outside of their own are their greatest opportunity for growth—thus preventing them from learning from well-meant tips and hints or trying out useful new strategies.

In addition, being self-centered fuels a higher opinion of oneself than reality justifies. In Prospecting we already discussed the ghost of false uniqueness—the one that deceives salespeople into believing that they are unique and special—which is just another way of saying that salespeople are a little too high on themselves.

Because salespeople perceive themselves as unique and special, they tend to be overly optimistic about their abilities and future performance. This includes the volume of referrals they expect to receive from customers as recognition of their greatness. Rather than relying on well-thought-out plans to steer referrals in their direction, salespeople tend to assume referrals will come based on their innate special qualities. After all, why would you need a referral plan if you are just that good, right?

These challenges—focus on self and excessive optimism—are chief among the reasons salespeople struggle with growing and asking for referrals, and they are the stock in trade of the self-centered ghosts: *egocentric bias* and *optimism bias*.

EGOCENTRIC BIAS

Being self-centered is not necessarily a bad thing. In fact, one could argue that humanity may not have evolved at all without a healthy level of self-centeredness.

Egocentric thinking—being self-centered—promotes self-esteem and encourages us to think highly of ourselves, to believe that we are good and worthy, which is as useful today as it was for our ancestors thousands of years ago. After all, if we do not believe we are valuable and worthy enough to survive, we are less likely to be motivated to do so.

Back in Prospecting, in the specific context of the false uniqueness bias, we introduced the behavioral science concept of the egocentric bias. As you will recall from that discussion, the egocentric bias persists because it magnifies a person's individual role in the experiences they have. As well as contributing to our desire to survive and reproduce, this was evolutionarily beneficial to our ancestors because it made our memories more personally relevant and easier for our brains to recall.

Think of the sports fan who is able to recall the pivotal moment that changed the course of a big game in painstaking detail because it coincided with the moment that they put on (or took off) their lucky shirt. Although in reality their choice of clothing had no impact on the outcome of the game whatsoever,[154] their egocentric bias sure did enhance their memory of the event.

Unfortunately, this way of thinking also distorts our perception of reality, giving each of us a more prominent role in the experiences we have than reality justifies. This distortion is why we are so focused on ourselves—putting ourselves at the center of the universe—and why we rely too much on our own perspective while underestimating other people's point of view.

Disregard for perspectives outside of our own can sometimes be perceived as a strength of conviction in what we think or believe. However, this perception prevents salespeople (and plenty of other humans) from hearing valuable feedback—good, bad, or otherwise—that could help them grow. Although disregarding what others think may keep an individual feeling strong and superior in the short term, ignoring alternative perspectives limits how much growth they can realize over the long term, whether it be in their personal understanding of sales, in their portfolio, or in their life.

By removing the egocentric bias's rose-colored glasses, we are able to see the self-centered approach to sales for what it really is: weakness disguised as strength.

---

154   If that were how sports really worked, the Warriors never would have lost to the Cavs in game seven of the 2016 NBA Finals.

Being self-centered is a terrible way to achieve our goals and get better. In fact, it is a great way to hold ourselves back from reaching our full potential—from growing. If salespeople close themselves off from other perspectives on the world and remain self-centered, they are closing themselves off from the greatest source of growth and transformation in their lives, necessarily limiting their growth and development.

Think of something that you are really good at. Whatever it may be—a sport, a subject in school, cooking, a card game, playing an instrument, building something—I am willing to bet you did not learn how to do or get good at that thing all by yourself. Everything you know and are good at has been, in some way, the distilled product of other people's perspectives. Each of us have parental figures and teachers and coaches and managers and mentors to thank for all of the knowledge that we claim as our own.

It is important for salespeople—and all people—to recognize that everything we know we learned from someone else. In fact, we already talked about this fundamental truth at the very beginning of our journey.

In the introduction we discussed the social brain hypothesis, which states that our ancestors developed larger brains as they became more social and began to share information with one another. In other words, as human beings evolved, being open to perspectives outside of our own made us smarter as individuals, as well as more effective and productive in group settings. By sharing, rather than each individual learning solely through trial and error, our ancestors accelerated their growth by learning from each other and building on each other's achievements.

If we remain closed to others' viewpoints and persist in viewing them as inferior, our growth is limited to the incremental addition of our own direct efforts. **Only by opening ourselves to the perspectives and wisdom of others are we able to compound our own direct efforts and grow exponentially.** It does not take a math whiz to appreciate that compounding is a faster path to growth than incremental addition.

The best way to manage the self-centered tendency that we are all drawn toward is awareness.

Simply being aware of the natural inclination to think first of yourself loosens the egocentric bias's grip on your mind, enabling you to steer yourself away from becoming too self-centered. Just by acknowledging your own egocentric bias, you take the biggest step toward recognizing that other perspectives are just as valuable your own, and open yourself to life's greatest source of growth.

In addition to limiting growth, perceiving others and what they have to offer as inferior to you and what you already know explains much of the substantial gap between the proven power of referrals to accelerate sales growth and salespeople's demonstrated lack of interest in pursuing them. Specifically, being self-centered also promotes an optimism bias—our second self-centered ghost in the machine.

OPTIMISM BIAS

According to behavioral science, by definition, the optimism bias causes people to believe that they themselves are less likely to experience a negative event than circumstance or facts would suggest. In effect, this translates to assuming that, in general, things will work out in your favor.

From an egocentric point of view—seeing oneself as unique and special—having an optimism bias makes perfect sense. *Of course things will work out, look how rad I am!*

As with all the other ghosts we have been discussing, the optimism bias does have evolutionarily beneficial functions. First, being optimistic provides a sense of control over a chaotic and often unpredictable world. Defaulting to seeing the glass half full keeps us from lingering too long and spending too much time and energy on all the things that could go wrong.

Second, being optimistic is better for our mental health. Mental stress—especially the chronic variety that comes with defaulting toward pessimism—takes a physical toll by overworking the nervous system. Therefore, over the course of a lifetime, optimists tend to be more mentally and physically fit than pessimists.[155] This makes intuitive sense, as optimists are more likely to get back up after they get knocked down, more likely to persist in the face of challenges and setbacks, than those with a pessimistic outlook.[156]

Lastly, optimists tend to outperform pessimists. Research done by economists Heifetz and Spiegel[157] shows that when a pessimist and an optimist are pitted against one another, the optimists drive the interaction, making them more aggressive and dominant.

Salespeople are nothing if not optimists. They have to be.

---

155   "Optimism and Your Health," Harvard Health Publishing, July 27, 2020, https://www.health.harvard.edu/heart-health/optimism-and-your-health.
156   Lise Solberg Nes and Suzanne C. Segerstrom, "Dispositional Optimism and Coping: A Meta-analytic Review," *Personality and Social Psychology Review* 10, no. 3 (August 2006): 235–51.
157   Aviad Heifetz and Yossi Spiegel, "On the Evolutionary Emergence of Optimism," *Social Science Research Network* (October 2000).

Having a bias toward optimism empowers salespeople to maintain an upbeat attitude when grinding through the low-probability game that is prospecting, which is essentially a prerequisite for success. However, the not-so-silver-lining of being a committed optimist is that salespeople expect that good things will happen without any directed effort on their part.

In reality, most salespeople are no better or worse than other salespeople. They are not unique and special. The rarity with which referrals are volunteered by customers unprompted—only 29% of the time—provides confirmation of this fact.

Left unchecked, the optimism bias leads salespeople to believe that help in the form of referrals will passively arrive. In reality, this just does not happen—highlighted by the Texas Tech research showing a 54% gap between customers' willingness to provide referrals and their likelihood to volunteer them unprompted. **A salesperson with a tendency toward excessive optimism will invariably find that the reality of the referrals they receive falls short of their expectations, as with their expectations of business growth.**

Our good friend Daniel Kahneman proposes two different ways of mitigating the exaggerated belief in self caused by the optimism bias.[158] First, challenge your optimistic assumptions with objective evidence. Look for base rates—relevant data points—that you may use to anchor your assumptions about performance, rather than using your optimistic opinions of yourself. Base rates are a form of awareness, which can take the wind out of the optimism bias's sails just as it does with the egocentric bias.

158   Daniel Kahneman, *Thinking, Fast and Slow* (New York: Farrar, Straus and Giroux, 2011), 265.

For example, instead of anticipating that referrals will simply come to you if you perform well, use statistics, like the one I discussed above from Texas Tech, as your base rate assumption and adjust your referral-gathering efforts accordingly. These objective measures make it plain that holding exaggerated expectations in terms of how many referrals you will get without asking is a good way to hold yourself back from realizing your growth goals.

Second, Kahneman suggests taking a "premortem" approach. As he describes it, a premortem is attempting to view a process from start to finish before it begins, being thoughtful about what is likely to happen, and objectively considering each decision point before becoming emotionally invested.[159]

For our purposes in discussing referrals, we will reframe Kahneman's approach as simply having a process focus— which should sound familiar to you.

———

In case you had not already recognized, the self-centered ghosts—egocentric bias and optimism bias—are cousins to the deceitful ghosts we met in Prospecting, connected in their focus on the self. However, although these types of ghosts are closely related, salespeople need to approach the self-centered ghosts much differently than they do the deceitful ghosts. The key difference in dealing with the haunts that hold back your growth is in recognizing the best use of your time and energy.

In Prospecting, we focused on circumventing the deceitful

---

159   To be clear, Kahneman's premortem is specifically focused on assuming something went wrong in regards to a project or decision-making process, and then working backwards to identify all the things that could have caused the failure.

ghosts that lead salespeople to believe they are *so* different that the rules of prospecting do not apply to them. Although there is merit in tackling those ghosts head-on, working around them is the path of least resistance. Circumventing the deceitful ghosts saves much-needed time and energy for playing the prospecting numbers game, which is the foundation of success for all types of sales.

Conversely, when we are striving to open ourselves for personal growth and generate sustainable business growth, we need to challenge the self-centered ghosts head-on. This begins with gaining awareness of them and their effects on you—which now you have.

But awareness is just the first step; the next, and the next after that, will be putting time and energy into challenging the effects of the self-centered ghosts. This is the path to growth; there is no circumventing it. That is what being heroic is all about.

EVEN HEROES GET A LITTLE HELP

> *"Becoming is better than being."*
> *—Carol Dweck*

If you want to fulfill your potential as a salesperson and follow the path of your own hero's journey, you have to follow in the footsteps of Gilgamesh, Roger Federer, and heroes of all shapes and sizes. You, like them, will have to challenge your self-centered nature in order to move forward through the obstacles life throws at you, embracing growth and change.

Both in sales and in life, when you come to a point of transformation, you must show a willingness to let go of the way you have always done things so that you may embrace the new, that you may evolve, adapt, and grow.

Embracing the hero's journey means becoming aware of your egocentric bias so that you may loosen its grip on you and embrace a new mindset: a mindset that frames openness to others, and accepting help, as something to invite rather than something to hide from.

In Prospecting, during our discussion of process focus, we teased something called the growth mindset. Here, in Growing, we will fully unpack the concept of growth mindset and apply it as the antidote to the fixed mindset endorsed by the egocentric bias.

FIXED VERSUS GROWTH MINDSET

As outlined by Stanford University education professor Carol Dweck in her best-selling book Mindset, *there are two types of mindsets: a* fixed *mindset and a* growth mindset.[160]

People with a fixed mindset believe that abilities are carved in stone—that who you are is who you are, period. A fixed mindset says that characteristics such as intelligence, personality, and creativity are static traits, and if you are not initially gifted with the ability to do something, then you are doomed to be a failure at that thing.

On the other hand, people with a growth mindset believe that abilities are things that may be cultivated through effort. A growth mindset says that everyone can change and grow through application and experience; that success is found in learning and improving.

160   Carol S. Dweck, *Mindset: The New Psychology of Success* (New York: Random House, 2006).

> *Having a fixed mindset creates an urgency to prove yourself over and over—Criticism is seen as an attack on your character and something to be avoided at all costs. Conversely, having a growth mindset encourages learning and effort and frames—criticism as valuable feedback—something to be embraced.*
>
> *The fixed mindset is about trying to be perfect—while the growth mindset is about learning and making progress.*

As you will recall from our "focus on the process" discussion in Prospecting, with a fixed mindset, your confidence is tied to outcomes rather than the process of getting better, and therefore it is more easily undermined by setbacks— reinforcing a negative feedback loop and the perception that your innate, fixed abilities are not good enough.

According to Professor Dweck, the hallmark of the growth mindset is the passion for getting better and sticking with it, especially when things are not going well. For example, almost without exception, those salespeople who persist with their cold-calling efforts despite the odds of success being stacked against them do so by embracing a growth mindset.

Your mindset will also dictate your reaction to changes in your company's procedures, whether they be product and service offerings, organizational reporting structures, or territory segmentation and selling parameters. Those salespeople with a fixed mindset are likely to wrestle with these changes and preemptively look to blame them for any future struggles or failures. On the other hand, those salespeople with a growth mindset will largely be able to accept such changes, whether good or bad, and focus on learning how to succeed in the new environment.

It is important to acknowledge that having a fixed or growth mindset is not binary—you are not limited to one or the other. Over time, based on their personal experiences, individuals are likely to maintain a growth mindset in some areas of their life and adopt a fixed mindset in others. Whatever mindset you have in a particular area will guide you when making decisions in that area.

The inherent duality of fixed and growth mindsets reminds me of an ancient parable, variously attributed to the Cherokee or Lenape, about two wolves.

> *A grandfather was teaching his grandson about life...*
>
> *"A fight is going on inside me," he said to the boy. "It is a terrible fight between two wolves.*
>
> *"One is arrogant, insecure, and full of self-doubt. The other is humble, empathetic, and confident.*
>
> *"This same fight is going on inside you—and inside every other person, too."*
>
> *The grandson thought about it for a minute and then asked his grandfather, "Which wolf will win?"*
>
> *The old man simply replied, "The one you feed."*

In this case, the arrogant, insecure, self-doubting wolf is a good description of the fixed mindset; the humble, empathetic, confident wolf represents the growth mindset.

Which mindset will you feed? Which mindset will guide you in your efforts throughout the sales cycle?

In order to grow—both in your business and in your personal life—you must cultivate a growth mindset. This is the conclusion of an expanding cohort of leaders of companies big and small, including Satya Nadella, CEO of Microsoft, who is transitioning the sprawling firm from a "know it all" (i.e., fixed) to a "learn it all" (i.e., growth) culture.[161]

In addition to keeping you focused on outcomes, a fixed mindset motivates you to focus more on yourself and, therefore, to underappreciate perspectives outside of your own. This self-centered focus reflects a more egocentric approach and holds you back from embracing input from others, from changing, from becoming the hero you are meant to be.

On the other hand, adopting a growth mindset encourages you to value and actively seek out other perspectives, while also remaining steadfast in the face of setbacks and challenges—reinforcing a positive feedback loop and the perception that *becoming* is better than *being*.

The importance of having a growth mindset is *the* master lesson of the hero's journey, and it may be the principal lesson humanity has been teaching itself at least since Gilgamesh was king.

Understanding that perspectives other than your own represent your greatest opportunity for improvement is the first step in embracing a growth mindset and directly challenging the egocentric biases that hold you back. Moreover, understanding the value of perspectives other than your own is also the first step in raising awareness of the optimism bias that leads you to think too highly of yourself and minimize the importance of receiving help from others.

---

161   Jessi Hempel, "Satya Nadella on Growth Mindsets: 'The Learn-It-All Does Better Than the Know-It-All," *Hello Monday* (blog), LinkedIn, December 9, 2019, https://www.linkedin.com/pulse/satya-nadella-growth-mindsets-learn-it-all-does-better-jessi-hempel/.

Heroes do not go it alone on their journeys. Help from a mentor is often the very thing the hero requires in order to find what they seek. Likewise, salespeople will need help on their journey if they hope to achieve the business growth they desire.

When I am struggling in my own life with being open to others and seeking out help, I am reminded of another parable.

> One day a father noticed his son trying to lift a heavy stone. Try as he might, the little boy could not lift the stone, becoming increasingly agitated after each failed attempt.
>
> After watching from afar for some time the father came to the boy and asked, "Are you using all your strength?"
>
> "Yes!" the boy cried.
>
> His father looked the boy in the eyes and said, "No, you are not. I have been right here waiting and you haven't asked for my help."

This little parable is a wonderful and powerful reminder that we do not have to go it alone—that asking for and receiving help makes our efforts more effective and more likely to succeed.

Stripping away the specific context of the sales cycle, what is the difference between asking for a referral and asking for help? To be blunt, there is none. **To ask for a referral is to ask for help. And in the context of growing your sales business, referrals are the most valuable help you can receive.**

As we discussed in the previous section, base rates—which in some ways can be viewed as a perspective other than our own—are a key tool in becoming aware of how the optimism bias drives our exaggerated expectations about passively receiving referrals. Now that we are aware of these exaggerated expectations, we need to shift our attention toward implementing a process that will ensure that we follow through on the need to proactively seek referrals.

In terms of day-to-day practice, thinking through and planning out how and when you will ask for a referral is the most important change you can make when it comes to combating the optimism bias that expects referrals will simply come to you. Specifically, you need to make referral requests a formal part of your sales process.

Salespeople need to integrate referral requests into their presentations and other client communications—when appropriate, of course. I mean this quite literally: the referral request needs to be inserted or outlined as a section of your agenda or presentation (your copy, not your prospect's), just like the key points you would never forget to highlight about your product or service or the cost-benefit analysis you are probably already sharing with your prospects.

We will discuss the specific timing of referrals in just a bit. But first, you should know that by taking steps to ensure that you will be asking for referrals, you are practically guaranteed an increase in the volume of referrals you will actually receive. This will, in turn, increase your ability to realize those sought-after leaps in performance.

It is fitting that, at the end of our journey, we will have come full circle—another common hero's journey trope—and find ourselves right back where we started: focusing on the process.

At the beginning of our journey, we leveraged a process focus to circumvent the deceitful ghosts and more effectively play the prospecting numbers game. Now, at the end, we will leverage the process focus to challenge the exaggerated expectations of the optimism bias to better leverage the power of referrals in accelerating our growth.

Now that we have an idea about the importance of the growth mindset and process focus in challenging the self-centered ghosts, all we need is a simple and effective tool that will guide us in implementing these changes.

MAKE A COMMITMENT

> *"Little things make big things happen."*
> *—John Wooden*

To kick this dead horse one more time, if you do not ask for referrals, you are going to receive very few—far less than you need to achieve the big leaps in growth that you deserve. Like it or not, the vast majority of people are not going to go out of their way to volunteer a referral to you. But, importantly, most of those same people are happy to provide you with a referral if you ask for one.

Armed with this knowledge, you just need some sort of mechanism to bridge this gap. That mechanism is a commitment.

Robert Cialdini, best-selling author of *Influence*, says that gaining commitments from others, no matter how small, is one of the best persuasion tools a salesperson has.

Commitments leverage what he calls the *consistency principle*, which simply states that people have a strong psychological need to be consistent with prior acts and statements they have done or made.[162]

Before behavioral science formally codified this phenomenon, it was broadly known in sales circles as the foot-in-the-door technique. Named after the door-to-door salesmen who developed it, the foot-in-the-door technique builds on small commitments—like permitting a salesperson to literally get their foot in the door and continue the conversation inside your house—to establish bigger commitments, with the biggest being an agreement to purchase something.

In the context of asking for referrals, your foot in the door is a commitment now from your customer for a referral in the future, with the future referral itself being the larger commitment you really want. In other words, the small thing (the commitment to give a referral) makes the big thing (the referral itself) happen.

To maximize the odds that you will get that commitment for a future referral, you need to know how and when to ask.

The best way to ask for commitment for a referral is with a simple *If/When-Then* statement. For example, "If I provide you X, will you provide me with a referral?" or "If you are satisfied with X, will you be willing to give me a referral?" *If or when I do something, then will you do something in return?*

Importantly, these statements communicate that you are not just asking a favor; they say that you will continue

---

162   Robert B. Cialdini, *Influence: The Psychology of Persuasion* (New York: HarperCollins, 2007).

providing value, reassuring the customer that they are being taken care of while also priming the consistency principle via their commitment to provide a referral once that value is delivered.

The most opportune time to wedge these If/When-Then statements into the sales process is right after the moment of purchase, as the negotiating phase wraps and the contract has just been signed, but before implementation or delivery begins. Studies by psychologists Leon Festinger and James Carlsmith have illustrated that people are most likely to champion something right after they have purchased it.[163]

Asking for a commitment to provide a referral right after the deal is consummated not only lowers the bar for commitment—thereby increasing the odds that the new customer will follow through on providing a referral in the future—but also provides time for the salesperson to prove their worth during implementation.

Further, it is a good idea to put some space between the If/When-Then statement and the actual request for a referral. Letting some time pass between the small thing (the commitment to give a referral) and the larger thing (the referral) allows the consistency principle to properly marinate in the mind of your customer and increases the likelihood that the larger thing you want will be received.

Lastly, bake your If/When-Then statement into the formal process of following up after a purchase, before implementation or delivery begins, and you will maximize the odds

163   Leon Festinger and James M. Carlsmith, "Cognitive Consequences of Forced Compliance," *Journal of Abnormal and Social Psychology* 58 (1959), 203–10.

that your new customer will provide you with the referral you need to realize the leaps in growth you deserve.

BONUS: THE RETURN

The hero's final act, after they have embraced growth and made a change in their life, is to return and share what they have learned with the world—to give back.

The same must be true for sales heroes. In particular, the sales hero must return the value they hope to receive from their prospects. Asking for help and receiving help is not a one-way street; referrals are a classic case of getting out what you put in.

Referrals are valuable to you. Therefore, you need to figure out ways to help and bring value to the person you would like a referral from.

From the time you first engage with a prospect in the prospecting phase, into the relationship-building phase, through affecting change and negotiating, during the onboarding process that converts that prospect into a customer, and for as long as you enjoy a professional relationship with that customer—at every step in the sales cycle—you need to be providing that person with value. This is all the more true if you hope to receive a referral from them at some point.

Put more simply, referrals are earned by providing value.

Before asking for either a commitment for a referral or the referral itself, ask yourself, "Have I provided enough value that, if I were standing in the customer's shoes, *I* would commit to that request?"

Providing value fundamentally drives at the universal ethic

of reciprocity and fairness that we discussed in the bonus section of Negotiating—doing unto others as you would have them do unto you, or, even better, doing unto others as *they* would have *you* do unto *them*. Providing value to your prospects justifies asking for something of value—like a referral—in return.

In the context of our growth discussion, cultivating both a growth mindset and a process focus will help you bring value to your prospects and customers.

Additionally, embracing a growth mindset and improving yourself personally and professionally is one of the best ways for you as a salesperson to provide value to your customers. Improving yourself creates a virtuous cycle. As you get better—and you will—you become more valuable. As you become more valuable, more people will want to work with you. As more people want to work with you, you have more opportunities to learn and grow, which will help you improve yourself. And so on.

The process focus also provides its own value by ensuring that commitments to provide value are actually delivered upon. Without a process and tools like If/When-Then statements to initiate the delivery of value, you run the risk of deprioritizing the value you must deliver to your customers—which will ultimately make you less effective and lower the odds that you will receive the referrals you need to reach your growth goals.

Using If/When-Then statements as you close your deals avoids this pitfall, ensuring that you will provide value by requiring you to commit to serving the customer *before* you receive something in return. While it may seem like a risk, a gesture of good faith such as this is a powerful building block of trust, reciprocity, and customer satisfaction.

When it comes down to it, the punchline of the hero's return is simply this: you get out what you put in.

———

Being a professional salesperson is a perpetually challenging, and at times exhausting, endeavor. Throughout your career—no matter your ability or your amount of experience—you will hear *no* exponentially more often than you will hear *yes*, and your wins will come few and far between your losses. So, when you hear one of those relatively rare *yes*es, make sure you take some time to smell the roses.

As a salesperson, converting prospects into customers is your job. While you are and will certainly be tasked with other responsibilities, your main purpose will always be to find and bring in new business. By successfully navigating the sales cycle and reaching this point—circumventing, connecting with, mitigating, and disarming all those behavioral ghosts that were lying in wait, programmed to interfere with your efforts—you have done your job.

But your work is not yet done. Because, for better or worse, there is no finish line in this race. If you want to realize the sustained success you deserve, you must follow in the footsteps of all the heroes that came before you, from Gilgamesh to Roger Federer and everyone in between.

Like all heroes, you must answer the call to adventure. And, when your moment of transformation comes, you must open up to a new way of doing things, letting go of the old and embracing change as the new way forward. Finally, after you have been transformed, you must then bring back what you have learned, sharing value with others.

The lesson of the sales hero's journey is to embrace a growth mindset.

In addition, like all heroes, you will need to accept help from others if you are to succeed in making a transformation and realizing your growth goals. You need to let go of the excessive optimism that encourages you to go it alone and to embrace asking for help, and then implement a process that ensures you follow through.

And although growing is the final phase of the sales cycle, it is not the end.

Growing is rather like the last portion of a lap in a race. As you approach what seems like the end, you recognize that you in fact are approaching a new beginning, arriving right back where your journey started. And just as the hero will reach many points of transformation in their lifetime, so too will you come back to the lessons presented here in Growing. **With each lap of the sales cycle you complete, you take another step forward, another step toward becoming the hero you are meant to be.**

CONCLUSION

There are few things in this world as awesome as surfing. Dropping into a wave and gliding up and down its face as it peels off in your wake is exhilarating. However, the price you have to pay to experience that exhilaration is no joke.

When I was in my twenties, learning how to surf was at the very top of my bucket list. Although that feels like a lifetime ago, I can still remember my first attempt like it was yesterday.

When I got to the shoreline, I made a cursory scan of the water to see where the other surfers were lined up. Then, not wanting to waste any time, I impatiently tossed my board into the water, flopped down onto it, and started paddling out in a straight line toward them. Little did I know, I was about to get a crash course in how to make surfing as difficult as possible. Literally.

Do not let the chill most surfers possess fool you. Surfing is hard. Like, really hard.

There are several critical components that you must master in order to experience the nirvana that is floating across the unblemished face of a wave. The component parts of positioning, timing, and execution are prerequisite to actually catching and riding a wave, and—as with anything worth learning—they take countless hours of concentrated effort to master.

But before you can even attempt to do any of that, first you have to get past the break.[164]

GETTING PAST THE BREAK

As I paddled out that very first time, it did not take long for a violent wall of whitewater to come barreling toward me. Knowing no better options, I steeled myself for impact. My crash course was about to begin.

I got absolutely hammered by that first wave. I was dislodged from my board, rag-dolled around underwater, and pushed back toward the beach. But after resurfacing, I caught my breath, gathered my board, regrouped, and started paddling back toward the other surfers.

Another wall of whitewater approached. Again, I was pummeled. Again, I regrouped. More whitewater. More pounding. Again. And again. And again.

A relentless succession of waves erased any progress I was able to make, depleting my energy and deflating my spirit. Eventually, after what felt like a thousand waves, the ocean mercifully relented from throwing haymakers at me and I

---

164   The zone where the waves break, delineated by the rows of whitewater rolling toward the shore.

finally made it past the break. Elated, but completely spent, I sat on my board for the next hour, watching everyone else surf. I tried a few times to muster the burst of energy needed to actually catch a wave, but I was out of gas.

In between failed attempts, with no better idea what to do, I looked back toward the beach and took notice of the way other surfers were paddling out to the lineup.[165]

The other surfers did not head straight into the break as I had. Instead, they entered the water well clear of the area where the waves were breaking, paddling around the violence I had suffered through and only turning toward the lineup once they were past the worst of it. From my new vantage point in the lineup, I also observed that other incoming surfers seemed to be able to consistently time their approach during a period of calm, often making it out to the lineup with nary a wall of whitewater to deal with.

These two observations comprised the first of many lessons I learned the hard way on my journey from ignorant kook to marginally capable surfer.

Waves break in the same place.[166] A seasoned surfer will tell you to avoid that place when paddling out. Instead, you want to look for a channel to one side or the other of a break, which will provide a much less violent path on your way out to the lineup.

A seasoned surfer will also tell you that waves come in sets.[167] Although each has its own unique rhythm, every

---

165   The takeoff point in which surfers cluster as they wait for waves to arrive.
166   This is specifically true of reef breaks and point breaks. Beach breaks may shift around a bit, but they will still generally break in the same area, or at least the same area on a specific day.
167   In truth, the behavior of groups of waves is not entirely predictable. However, there are patterns to groups of waves that, while not statistically replicable, do work for surfers.

surf break has a consistent pattern. Recognizing that pattern before paddling out enables you to time your entry and approach to the lineup during the lull in between sets, making the work of getting out to the lineup a hell of a lot easier.

These two nuggets of wisdom are arguably the most important pieces of advice for a beginner surfer. Unfortunately, before paddling out on that maiden session, I knew neither.

Had I known more, my initial surfing experience would have been *a lot* more enjoyable. But because I did not understand how the ocean works, when I first paddled out, I inadvertently took the path of *most* resistance, taking the whole experience from a challenging pursuit to an overwhelmingly exhausting one.

After the trauma of my initial experience, and after observing other surfers, my subsequent attempts at surfing were much more productive and enjoyable. Because I better understood how the ocean worked, I was able to find paths of *least* resistance when paddling out—putting me on the path toward actual progress in learning how to surf.

In this way—understanding the difference between the path of most and the path of least resistance—sales and surfing are the same.

Both are challenging. Both require disciplined, consistent effort over time. Both are exhilarating when executed successfully. And both are made exponentially harder if you do not understand the key underlying dynamics that affect the entire endeavor.

In surfing, those dynamics literally lie underneath you in

the motion of the ocean. In sales, as we have discussed throughout this book, those underlying dynamics are the ghosts in the machine that push decision-makers away from the perfectly rational decision-making process that most salespeople and sales methodologies take as given.

THE PATH OF LESS RESISTANCE

> *"As to methods there may be a million and then some, but principles are few. The man who grasps principles can successfully select his own methods. The man who tries methods, ignoring principles, is sure to have trouble."*
> —Harrington Emerson

I will say it again: sales is hard. Fortunately, there is something you can do to make it less hard: accept, understand, and embrace human irrationality.

Approaching prospects and customers as though they are perfectly rational when making decisions—especially decisions about change—represents a misunderstanding of how the human mind actually approaches decisions.

When we are attempting to affect change—which, as salespeople, is exactly what we are trying to do—the purely rational approach endorsed, implicitly or otherwise, by so many sales methodologies is the path of *most* resistance.

Like a surfer unaware of the underlying dynamics that guide the motion of the ocean, unwittingly heading straight into the violence of the break, a salesperson who approaches prospects without an understanding of the underlying dynamics that guide human decision-making is going to make their own job much harder.

Without an understanding of the irrationalities that affect decision-making, salespeople's effectiveness in mitigating their prospects' innate resistance to change will be compromised. Further, their chosen sales methodologies, no matter how great, will be limited in their ability to deliver results.

Understanding that prospects are not the perfectly rational *Homo economicus* they are often assumed to be provides a more accurate view of the sometimes-irrational human beings they actually are. Further, embracing behavioral science principles will help us better understand and connect with our prospects and customers, which will in turn enable us to more effectively affect change.

The behavioral science principles and tools outlined in this book present you with a tremendous opportunity to differentiate yourself from your peers. **Overlaying these principles on top of your preferred sales methodology provides you with a path of *least* resistance and makes your job easier—not easy, of course, but easi*er*. In addition, this deeper understanding of decision-making will accelerate your learning curve, unleash your creativity and unique talents, and make whatever sales methodology you embrace work better for *you*.**

All else equal, applying a better understanding of humanity's behavioral quirks to your sales efforts will tip the scales in your favor and increase your odds of success, no matter your chosen sales methodology.

These insights can only take your sales career further, and understanding them has the added benefit of enabling you to better parse human behavior in almost all contexts, from sales to politics to personal relationships.

However, understanding alone is not enough to realize success. This book can only help you so much if you do not take action on what you have learned. Like most things in life, in order to bear fruit, the guidance and recommendations provided in this book require consistent repetition over time.

GET YOUR REPS IN

"Knowing it is not as good as
putting it into practice."
—*Xun Kuang*

If you want to get good at a thing, you have to practice doing that thing.

Want to get good at cooking food? You have to practice cooking food. Want to get good at shooting a basketball? You have to practice shooting a basketball. Want to get good at math? You have to practice doing math. Want to get good at speaking a foreign language? You have to practice speaking that language. Want to get good at lifting weights? You have to practice lifting weights.

Nobody is born being good at anything.[168] If someone has expertise in something, it is primarily because they have practiced doing that thing *a lot*.

Repetition is a proven means of building expertise. However, repetition alone is not enough to develop expertise; repeating the same ineffective techniques over and over

---

168   *Of course* some people start with innate talents that others don't have, but do not mistake a jump start for being good. Bobby Flay did not spring from the womb with the ability to cook another chef's signature dish better than they can. Sure, he probably has some innate talents in the kitchen that amplify his ability, but he is that good at cooking because he has spent a lifetime practicing cooking.

again leads, reliably, to a dead end. To be effective, repetition must be targeted at what works and channeled through a proven and repeatable methodology.

Chefs have French technique. Basketball players have shooting form drills. Math students have PEMDAS exercises. Foreign language learners have the grammar-translation method. Weightlifters have progressive overload.

Fortunately, salespeople are spoiled for choice when it comes to repeatable methodologies.

As we have discussed throughout this book, there is a wide variety of proven go-to-market sales methods by which a salesperson may choose to channel their efforts. To get good at sales, an individual or organization needs to commit to a sales method and apply it consistently and repetitively over time.

As we conclude our journey, it is important to mention that the biggest mistake those in search of expertise—including salespeople—make is giving up on a methodology prematurely.

When a newly applied methodology or process does not provide instant benefit, people are quick to draw the conclusion that the methodology or process does not work—when, in reality, that person simply did not give that methodology or process the consistent application and repetition it needed to work its magic.

To expect a method or process to deliver results overnight is to mismanage your expectations. **Even proven methodologies require sustained application before they become truly worthwhile. Likewise, the behavioral science tools offered in this book will *not* bring instant results.**

Apply these insights intermittently, or give up on them because they do not radically improve your performance overnight, and you are unlikely to realize their benefits. In fact, that is a good way to stay right where you are.

On the other hand, with consistent and repetitive application over time, overlaying these insights on top of your chosen sales methodology will significantly enhance your efforts, help you develop a deeper level of expertise as a salesperson, and tip the scales of success in your favor.

A LOOK BACK

> *"Even the most analytical thinkers are predictably irrational; the really smart ones acknowledge and address their irrationalities."*
> —Dan Ariely

On our journey though the sales cycle, we have covered a lot of ground and dug into some pretty heady concepts. If pressed to summarize the behavioral view of the sales cycle as presented in Ghosts in the Machine in as few words as possible, I would do so thusly.

- Build a foundation for success (Prospecting)
- Make friends (Relationship Building)
- Reframe the story (Changing)
- Seek better outcomes (Negotiating)
- Focus on getting better (Growing)

Rinse and repeat.

A more robust accounting of our journey reveals the seven types of ghosts in the machine that we encountered— those categories of behavioral irrationalities that have the greatest effect on decision-making in the sales process—as well as the behavioral tools we can learn to use in managing them.

PROSPECTING

In Prospecting we encountered the deceitful ghosts—fear of rejection, false uniqueness, and procrastination—and learned how to circumvent them with a process focus and SMART goals.

Prospecting is an unrelenting numbers game. How many cold calls you make is the single most important factor in determining how many relationships you are able to establish—and how many subsequent sales you are able to close—and the deceitful ghosts make it triply hard to get that crucial calling volume.

Instead of getting discouraged, focus on the process, not the outcome. It is important to remember that a low probability of success on any given call is to be expected and is not a reflection of your ability or worth.

Whether you are sitting down on day one of your first sales job or midway through your sales career, take the time right now to define your SMART—Specific, Measurable, Achievable, Relevant, and Time-Bound—prospecting goals. Use the principles of the scientific method to guide your efforts, testing your methods to see which produce results, and keep iterating until you are able to consistently achieve your goals.

Start by determining your revenue goal. Once you have established (or been told) your revenue goal, determine how many deals you need to close to reach that revenue goal, then extrapolate back from there. How many proposals do you need to issue to close that many deals? How many meetings do you need to participate in to get to that many proposals? Finally, how many prospects do you need to contact over a given period of time in order to reach the necessary number of meetings?

You will have to make some assumptions in determining the exact number of deals, prospects, etc., especially if you are starting from scratch; these should be informed by your own experience and market knowledge, any insights provided by your company, and research.

Do not worry if those assumptions turn out to be wrong. Initially, you just need a starting point. From there, faithful and iterative execution of the scientific method will reveal the principles that will guide you to consistent achievement of your goals, whatever they may be.

Remember, sales is an art, but it is just as much a science—a science that you are capable of harnessing.

RELATIONSHIP BUILDING

In Relationship Building we encountered the lazy ghosts— stereotyping and in-group bias—and learned how to connect with them through active listening, mirroring and matching, and the buyer-type chart.

Our relationship-building discussion in a nutshell: shut up and listen.

Above all else, your ability to build relationships with your prospects and customers hinges on your ability and willingness to actively listen. In the early stages of your relationship-building efforts, your value proposition matters far less than demonstrating that you understand and are sincerely interested in whatever your prospect is sharing with you—whether it is immediately relevant to what you are selling or not.

All things considered, human beings weight interpersonal factors more heavily than rational factors when they are making decisions. The best way to make selling easier is to become a professional friend—someone that your prospect actually *likes*. Practice the mirroring and matching techniques we discussed and become an expert in shifting GEARS—Gestures, Energy, Aspect, Rate, and Sound—as a means to meet your prospects where they are and better connect with them.

Do not attempt to leverage these tools as tricks to shortcut your way into a friendship; people have a way of sniffing out and rejecting such nakedly superficial posturing. Rather, use these tools in good faith, genuinely trying to understand the person in front of you and develop a relationship, and you will find yourself more easily accepted and your prospects and customers more willing to open up to you.

You also do well to commit the buyer-type chart we reviewed to memory. Being able to quickly assess the type of decision-maker you are dealing with—odds are they will be from the early or late majority—will help you better speak their language and frame your offerings in ways they are more likely to accept.

CHANGING

In Changing we encountered the fearful ghosts—loss aversion, the status quo bias, and confirmation bias—and the busy ghosts—the focusing illusion, the Einstellung effect, and choice overload—and learned to mitigate them with framing, priming, and storytelling.

Human beings fear change, and in most cases, we would much rather decide not to decide.

Whether in the form of a favorite entrée, cable TV, or a vendor providing a product or service for their business, people like the certainty of what they know. You, the enterprising salesperson, represent uncertainty. Therein lies the crux of the challenge you confront in your role as an agent of change.

Professional decision-makers spend much of their lives afraid of making bad choices and overwhelmed by modern life's demands on their attention. As such, when they are presented with alternatives to their current systems and processes, the fearful and busy ghosts in the machine loom large, encouraging them to think about it as little as possible, and, often, to decide not to decide.

When striving to affect change as a salesperson, you must continue listening to your prospects with a focus on understanding what is important to them and seeing the world through their eyes. Only with these insights can you frame your rational arguments around values that truly matter to your prospects.

Understanding the specific loss aversion, sunk cost bias, or regret avoidance that motivates a prospect's decision-making will enable you to frame your products or services both as means to that end and as mechanisms to give your prospects greater control over business performance.

Listening to understand what is really important to your prospects and customers also empowers you to elevate in attention, or prime, the beliefs your customers hold that may be positively associated with your products and services. Priming values that are already important to your prospects can help you cut through the noise and distraction assailing them and gain a foothold in their minds.

Perhaps the most powerful tool you have for affecting change is storytelling. Do not just regurgitate data points to your prospects. Instead, when presenting customer success stories and data points, tell your prospects a story, and remember to make them the hero.

Framing customer success stories around an understanding of the audience's wants and needs primes otherwise unassociated ideas in a package that people will remember—helping to mitigate the fearful and busy ghosts in one fell swoop.

NEGOTIATING

In Negotiating we encountered the competitive ghost—the zero-sum bias—and the stubborn ghost—anchoring—and learned to disarm them with collaboration and preparation.

While scientists and economists often make a big deal over humanity's competitive instincts, our collaborative instincts are just as powerful and deeply ingrained as our competitive ones.

If you find yourself at the negotiating table, your efforts in prospecting, relationship building, and affecting change have been successful, and you have most likely formed a pretty good connection with your prospect. Do not ruin that connection by suddenly seeing a competitor sitting across from you.

Sales and negotiating are not necessarily win-lose propositions; they are often infinite games that have better outcomes when you take a collaborative approach. Rather than competing with your negotiating counterparty and becoming entrenched in your respective positions, work with them to seek out win-win solutions that are focused on your respective interests.

Further, throughout your negotiations, be aware of the anchors that either you or your counterparty have set as reference points for the negotiation, whether they are prices or other boundaries. Anchors such as these can trigger the stubborn ghosts and derail your hard-earned progress.

Most importantly, realizing more optimal negotiated outcomes hinges on your preparation before the negotiation begins. Use our negotiation prep sheet to think through the key variables in advance of your negotiations so that you may better focus on establishing a collaborative tone once the negotiation begins.

GROWING

In Growing we encountered the self-centered ghosts—egocentric bias and optimism bias—and learned to challenge them in ourselves and others with a growth mindset, a process focus, and commitments.

Becoming is better than being, and embracing change and asking for help are foundational elements in compounding your growth.

Unfortunately, our innate self-centered perspective encourages us to think that the world revolves around us, to see ourselves as unique and special, and to focus on outcomes.

As your unique sales journey unfolds, it is critical that you challenge your egocentricity and meet your moments of transformation with a growth mindset, recognizing that you are no better or worse than anyone else and focusing on the process of getting better.

This is the theme of the hero's journey; make it the theme of your sales journey, and you will see both personal and sales career growth.

Throughout your sales career, it is also important to keep your optimistic instincts in check; they are a blessing and a curse. You need to be optimistic to survive the grind of the prospecting numbers game, but be careful that you aren't so optimistic that you expect people to fall over themselves just to work with you.

Overly optimistic feelings blind you to one of the best tools you have for maximizing your growth: help from others.

Proactively seeking out help from others—especially in the form of referrals—is the best way to realize your individual potential as a salesperson and accelerate the growth of your sales business. Referrals have the potential to grow your business faster than anything else. Do not leave them to chance; make them part of your process.

Referral requests are just as important to your success as any other single aspect of your communication with prospects and customers. Make asking for them a formal part of your presentation and meeting agendas, especially in the window of time immediately following a purchase. Incorporate If/When-Then statements into your pitch to gain a commitment from your new customer, and make your own commitment to deliver value to them so that you may earn their referral.

On your own you are only able to make incremental progress; with the help of others, your progress will be exponential.

———

When the behavioral rubber meets the proverbial sales road and you begin to apply these insights, it is important for you to remember that your goal is not to eliminate the ghosts in the machine that you encounter. These biases and behavioral quirks are too strong and too deeply ingrained in the human psyche.

Rather, your goal is to recognize and understand these ghosts—to be aware of them. Awareness, as we have discussed often in our journey through the sales cycle, is one of the best mitigants you have in managing the resistance created by these ghosts and keeping them from derailing your selling efforts.

Just like you, the people you are selling to are prone to irrationality. Leveraging insights from behavioral science will complement your chosen sales methodology, enhance it, and make it a lot more effective. **If you embrace this core message—and if you practice *a lot*—I am confident that you will have more success in the future than you have had in the past, no matter how impressive or how underwhelming your current level of success may be.**

If that is not a message worth embracing, I don't know what is.

Thank you for coming with me on this ride. I hope your newfound appreciation for the ghosts in the machine—all those decision-making irrationalities—will help you ease your way past the sales breaks that we all struggle with and allow you to have a lot more fun catching waves!

ONE MORE BONUS: RECOMMENDATIONS

One final bonus before we go.

Way back in the introduction I mentioned that in our exploration of biases and decision-making glitches, we stand on the shoulders of giants. I would be remiss if I did not point you in the direction of some of those giants.

Without further ado, I leave you with a list of book recommendations that represent much of the foundational knowledge that I have shared with you here. Enjoy!

- *Thinking, Fast and Slow* by Daniel Kahneman— What the Old Testament is to monotheistic religion, this book is to behavioral science.
- *Being Wrong* by Kathryn Schulz—This book unpacks all the reasons why human beings think they are always right.
- *Influence* and *Pre-suasion* by Robert Cialdini—No one has had more success translating behavioral science principles into practical application than psychologist and author Robert Cialdini; these two books deliver the lion's share of those practical applications.
- *Getting to Yes* by Roger Fisher, William Ury, and Bruce Patton—This is the best negotiations book I have ever read.
- *Mindset* by Carol S. Dweck—Whether you approach learning and intelligence with a fixed mindset or a growth mindset, you are right...but a growth mindset will take you further.

CALL TO ACTION

Thanks for joining me on this behavioral journey through the sales cycle. I hope you enjoyed it.

Now, I'd like to follow through on the commitment we made to each other at the end of the introduction. Do you remember?

If you believe I delivered on my promise to help you become aware of the ghosts in the machine, and if I provided a few nuggets of insight that you plan on leveraging in your sales journey, will you take five minutes right now, go to www.RyanVoeltz.com, and join the GitM mailing list?

If you will, then I will commit to providing you with even more behavioral insights that will help you on your sales journey. I hope you will. I'd love to stay in touch.

Cheers!

—RYAN VOELTZ

ACKNOWLEDGMENTS

This book did not happen without the tribe of people that helped me along the way.

Thank you to all the friends and family who read various drafts of this book and provided me with invaluable feedback. You challenged me to make this book better.

Thank you to Tim Flood and Alison Fragale, two of my favorite business school professors, for being exceptionally generous with your time and for providing such thoughtful advice. It was an unexpected bonus that this project provided the opportunity to spend time with both of you again. I hope similar opportunities present themselves in the future.

Thank you to John Cerqueira, my sales consulting mentor and overall rad dude, for making yourself available to a stranger. Your feedback and sales wisdom helped guide this book more than you know. As this little journey unfolds, I will continue to seek out excuses to pick your brain.

Thank you to PRESStinely's Kristen Wise and Maira Pedreira, my marketing and PR mavens, for holding my hand into and through the post-publishing jungle. The two of you are as enjoyable to work with as you are expert at what you do.

Thank you to Jack Walker, my graphic designer, for providing this book with a much-needed finishing touch. Breathing life into sales statistics and charts is no easy task, and you did so beautifully.

Thank you to Casey and Emily Fritz, my cover and interior designers, for making this book look and feel better than I ever thought it could. I'm lucky to have found the two of you.

Thank you to Scott Sugarman, my technical editor, for checking my logic in the application of these behavioral science principles, and for doing the dirty work of making sure everything has been properly cited and referenced. Your work on this book is as valuable as anyone's, including mine.

Most importantly, thank you to Phoenix Bunke, my editor. I could fill another book just singing your praises, and it still wouldn't be enough. It's been quite a journey and I am fortunate that I had you to share it with. From developmental editing—which this book needed *a lot* of—all the way through proofreading, you always overdelivered. I can't thank you enough and I will be forever grateful.

To all: thank you.

www.ingramcontent.com/pod-product-compliance
Lightning Source LLC
Chambersburg PA
CBHW071544210326
41597CB00019B/3110